everyday
wok & stir-fry

This is a Parragon book
First published in 2006

Parragon
Queen Street House
4 Queen Street
Bath BA1 1HE, UK

Copyright © Parragon Books Ltd 2006
Designed by Terry Jeavons & Company

ISBN 1-40548-684-8

Printed in China

This book uses imperial and metric measurements. Follow the same units of measurement throughout; do not mix imperial and metric. All spoon measurements are level, unless otherwise stated: teaspoons are assumed to be 5ml, and tablespoons are assumed to be 15ml. Unless otherwise stated, milk is assumed to be whole, eggs and individual fruits such as bananas are medium and pepper is freshly ground black pepper.

Recipes using raw or very lightly cooked eggs should be avoided by infants, the elderly, pregnant women, convalescents and anyone suffering from an illness. Pregnant and breast-feeding women are advised to avoid eating peanuts and peanut products.

everyday

wok & stir-fry

introduction

As you will soon see when you start cooking recipes from this book, buying a good wok is one of the best investments in kitchen equipment that you will ever make. This incredibly versatile pan can be used for soups, deep-frying, steaming and, most importantly, for stir-frying, the favourite cooking method of the people of Southeastern and Eastern Asia.

Wok cooking is ideal for anyone who is always on the go, because the dishes are nutritious, very quick and easy to prepare and cook, and absolutely delicious. Cooked rapidly over a high heat, vegetables retain their crisp texture and vibrant colour, so that

the visual appeal of a stir-fried dish matches its taste, and meat, poultry, fish, tofu or nuts add the protein. Wonderful sauces, made in advance and then stirred in to heat through before serving, add a finishing touch.

A traditional wok is made of steel, and when you get it home it will need a little preparation before use, known as 'seasoning'. First of all, scrub off the protective oiled coating in warm, soapy water, rinse well and let half dry. Next, stand the damp wok on a hob over low heat until it is completely dry. Drizzle in a little oil and wipe it round the inside with kitchen paper. Continue heating until the oil smokes and burns off, then repeat with another coating of oil. The wok will darken in colour and should never need scrubbing again, just wiping carefully.

You can prepare for wok and stir-fry cooking by buying in a few store-cupboard ingredients. Items such as rice and a variety of noodles, peanut, sesame and vegetable oils, coconut milk, soy

sauce, canned water chestnuts and straw mushrooms, fish sauce, curry pastes, spices and cornflour will get you started and all you'll need are the fresh ingredients to enable you to whip up a feast in moments.

Take to the wok and have fun!

soups &
appetizers

You might never have thought of making soup in a wok, but the people of Thailand and China do it all the time! Start with the classic Chicken Noodle Soup and you will soon discover the joys of the wonderful flavours and textures that go into soups from this part of the world. Coconut milk is sometimes used, giving a rich, creamy result, but often the soup is a simple broth of vegetables, usually with a little meat, poultry or fish added.

If you are a lover of Chinese and Thai food, you'll be pleased to find that some of your favourite appetizers – the ones that you are often tempted to buy in packets because they look complicated – are actually very quick and easy to make. Those delicious, crispy, little parcels that hold various tasty fillings – spring rolls, wontons and dumplings – take just a few minutes to construct and another couple of minutes to cook, and once you've tasted them fresh from the wok, well drained on kitchen paper, you'll never go back to buying them. Try making delicious Japanese tempura, too – vegetables cooked in a coating of crisp, light batter. When deep-frying, remember that the fat needs to stay really hot to give the best result, so cook in small batches and keep each batch warm as you cook the next.

chicken noodle soup

ingredients

SERVES 4–6

1 sheet dried egg noodles
   from a 250 g/9 oz packet

1 tbsp corn oil

4 skinless, boneless chicken
   thighs, diced

1 bunch of spring onions,
   sliced

2 garlic cloves, chopped

2-cm/³/4-inch piece fresh root
   ginger, finely chopped

850 ml/1¹/2 pints chicken
   stock

175 ml/6 fl oz coconut milk

3 tsp Thai red curry paste

3 tbsp peanut butter

2 tbsp light soy sauce

salt and pepper

1 small red pepper,
   dedeseeded and chopped

55 g/2 oz frozen peas

method

1 Place the noodles in a shallow heatproof dish and soak in boiling water according to the packet directions.

2 Meanwhile, heat the oil in a preheated wok. Add the chicken and stir-fry for 5 minutes, or until lightly browned. Add the white part of the spring onions, the garlic and root ginger and stir-fry for 2 minutes.

3 Add the stock, coconut milk, curry paste, peanut butter and soy sauce. Season to taste with salt and pepper. Bring to the boil, stirring constantly, then simmer for 8 minutes, stirring occasionally. Add the pepper, peas and green spring onion tops and cook for a further 2 minutes.

4 Drain the noodles, then add them to the wok and heat through. Spoon into warmed serving bowls and serve immediately.

duck with spring onion soup

ingredients

SERVES 4

2 duck breasts, skin on

2 tbsp Thai red curry paste

2 tbsp vegetable or peanut oil

bunch of spring onions,
  chopped

2 garlic cloves, crushed

5-cm/2-inch piece fresh
  root ginger, grated

2 carrots, sliced thinly

1 red pepper, deseeded and
  cut into strips

1 litre/1³/₄ pints chicken stock

2 tbsp sweet chilli sauce

3–4 tbsp Thai soy sauce

400 g/14 oz canned straw
  mushrooms, drained

method

1 Slash the skin of the duck 3 or 4 times with a sharp knife and rub in the curry paste. Cook the duck breasts, skin side down, in a wok over high heat for 2–3 minutes. Turn over, reduce the heat and cook for a further 3–4 minutes, until cooked through. Lift out and slice thickly. Set aside and keep warm.

2 Meanwhile, heat the oil in a wok and stir-fry half the spring onions, the garlic, root ginger, carrots and red pepper for 2–3 minutes. Pour in the stock and add the chilli sauce, soy sauce and mushrooms. Bring to the boil, reduce the heat and simmer for 4–5 minutes.

3 Ladle the soup into warmed bowls, top with the duck slices and garnish with the remaining spring onions. Serve immediately.

thai-style seafood soup

ingredients

SERVES 4

1.25 litres/2$^{1}/_{4}$ pints fish stock
1 lemon grass stalk, split
    lengthways
pared rind of $^{1}/_{2}$ lime or
    1 fresh kaffir lime leaf
2.5-cm/1-inch piece fresh
    root ginger, sliced
$^{1}/_{4}$ tsp chilli paste, or to taste
4–6 spring onions
200 g/7 oz large or medium
    raw prawns, peeled
salt
250 g/9 oz scallops (16–20)
2 tbsp coriander leaves
finely chopped red pepper or
    fresh red chilli rings,
    to garnish

method

1 Place the stock in a wok with the lemon grass, lime rind, root ginger and chilli paste. Bring just to the boil, then reduce the heat and simmer, covered, for 10–15 minutes.

2 Cut the spring onions in half lengthways, then slice crossways very thinly. Cut the prawns almost in half lengthways, keeping the tails intact. Devein if necessary.

3 Pour the stock through a sieve, then return to the wok and bring to a simmer, with bubbles rising at the edges and the surface trembling. Add the spring onions and cook for 2–3 minutes. Taste and season with salt, if needed. Stir in a little more chilli paste if wished.

4 Add the scallops and prawns and poach for 1 minute, or until they turn opaque and the prawns curl.

5 Drop in the coriander leaves, then ladle the soup into warmed serving bowls, dividing the shellfish evenly, and garnish with pepper or chilli rings.

sweetcorn & crab soup

ingredients

SERVES 4

2 tbsp vegetable or peanut oil

4 garlic cloves, chopped finely

5 shallots, chopped finely

2 lemon grass stalks,
    chopped finely

2.5-cm/1-inch piece fresh
    root ginger, chopped finely

1 litre/1³/₄ pints chicken stock

400 g/14 oz canned
    coconut milk

175 g/6 oz frozen sweetcorn
    kernels

350 g/12 oz canned
    crabmeat, drained
    and shredded

2 tbsp fish sauce

juice of 1 lime

1 tsp jaggery or soft light
    brown sugar

bunch of fresh coriander,
    chopped, to garnish

method

1 Heat the oil in a wok and sauté the garlic, shallots, lemon grass and root ginger over low heat, stirring occasionally, for 2–3 minutes or until softened.

2 Add the stock and coconut milk and bring to the boil. Add the sweetcorn, reduce the heat and simmer gently for 3–4 minutes.

3 Add the crabmeat, fish sauce, lime juice and sugar and simmer gently for 1 minute.

4 Ladle into warmed bowls, garnish with the chopped coriander and serve immediately.

spicy thai soup with prawns

ingredients

SERVES 4

2 tbsp tamarind paste

4 fresh red Thai chillies,
    very finely chopped

2 garlic cloves, crushed

2.5-cm/1-inch piece fresh
    galangal, very finely
    chopped

4 tbsp Thai fish sauce

2 tbsp palm sugar or
    caster sugar

8 fresh kaffir lime leaves,
    roughly torn

1 litre/1^3/$_4$ pints fish stock

115 g/4 oz very thinly sliced
    carrots

175 g/6 oz diced sweet
    potato

100 g/3^1/$_2$ oz baby corn cobs,
    halved

3 tbsp coriander, coarsely
    chopped

100 g/3^1/$_2$ oz cherry
    tomatoes, halved

225 g/8 oz cooked fantail
    prawns

method

1 Place the tamarind paste, chillies, garlic, galangal, fish sauce, sugar, lime leaves and stock in a large, preheated wok. Bring to the boil, stirring constantly.

2 Reduce the heat and add the carrots, sweet potato and baby corn cobs to the mixture in the wok.

3 Simmer the soup for 10 minutes or until the vegetables are just tender.

4 Stir the coriander, cherry tomatoes and prawns into the soup and heat through for 5 minutes.

5 Transfer the soup to warmed serving bowls and serve hot.

vegetable & noodle soup

ingredients

SERVES 4

2 tbsp vegetable or peanut oil

1 onion, sliced

2 garlic cloves, chopped finely

1 large carrot, cut into thin
   sticks

1 courgette, cut into thin
   sticks

115 g/4 oz broccoli, cut into
   florets

1 litre/1³/₄ pints vegetable
   stock

400 ml/14 fl oz coconut milk

3–4 tbsp Thai soy sauce

2 tbsp Thai red curry paste

55 g/2 oz wide rice noodles

115 g/4 oz mung or soy bean
   sprouts

4 tbsp chopped fresh
   coriander

method

1 Heat the oil in a wok and stir-fry the onion
and garlic for 2–3 minutes.

2 Add the carrot, courgette and broccoli and
stir-fry for 3–4 minutes, until just tender.

3 Pour in the stock and coconut milk and
bring to the boil. Add the soy sauce, curry
paste and noodles and simmer for 2–3
minutes, until the noodles have swelled.

4 Stir in the bean sprouts and coriander and
serve immediately.

mushroom & noodle soup

ingredients

SERVES 4

$^1/_2$ cucumber

2 tbsp vegetable oil

2 spring onions, finely chopped

1 garlic clove, cut into thin strips

125 g/4$^1/_2$ oz flat or open-cap mushrooms, thinly sliced

600 ml/1 pint water

25 g/1 oz Chinese rice noodles

$^3/_4$ tsp salt

1 tbsp soy sauce

method

1 Halve the cucumber lengthways. Scoop out the seeds using a teaspoon, then slice the flesh thinly.

2 Heat the oil in a large preheated wok. Add the spring onions and garlic and stir-fry for 30 seconds. Add the mushrooms and stir-fry for 2–3 minutes.

3 Stir in the water. Break the noodles into short lengths and add to the soup. Bring to the boil, stirring.

4 Add the cucumber slices, salt and soy sauce and simmer for 2–3 minutes.

5 Ladle the soup into warmed bowls, distributing the noodles and vegetables evenly.

rice noodles with tofu soup

ingredients

SERVES 4

200 g/7 oz firm tofu, drained
vegetable or peanut oil,
    for deep-frying
1 litre/1³/4 pints vegetable
    stock
5 spring onions, halved
1 yellow pepper, deseeded
    and sliced
2 celery stalks, sliced
1 small onion, sliced thinly
4 kaffir lime leaves
2 tbsp Thai soy sauce
1 tbsp Thai green curry paste
175 g/6 oz wide rice noodles,
    soaked and drained
chopped fresh coriander,
    to garnish

method

1 Using a sharp knife, cut the tofu into even cubes. Pour the oil into a wok to a depth of about 5 cm/2 in and heat. Deep-fry the tofu, in batches, until browned all over. Remove with a slotted spoon, drain on kitchen paper and set aside.

2 Pour the stock into the clean wok and bring to the boil. Add the spring onions, yellow pepper, celery, onion, lime leaves, soy sauce and curry paste, and simmer for 4–5 minutes. Add the noodles and the tofu and simmer for 2–3 minutes.

3 Ladle into warmed bowls and serve hot, topped with chopped coriander.

kara-age chicken

ingredients

SERVES 4

6 skinless, boneless
chicken thighs, about
100 g/3$^1/_2$ oz each

4 tbsp shoyu (Japanese
soy sauce)

4 tbsp mirin

2 tsp finely grated fresh
root ginger

2 garlic cloves, crushed

oil, for deep-frying

70 g/2$^1/_2$ oz potato flour or
cornflour

pinch of salt

lemon wedges, to serve

method

1 Cut the chicken into large cubes and put in a bowl. Add the soy sauce, mirin, root ginger and garlic and turn the chicken to coat well. Cover with clingfilm and marinate in a cool place for 20 minutes.

2 Preheat a wok, then fill one-third full with oil, or use a deep-fryer. Heat the oil to 180–190°C/350–375°F, or until a cube of bread browns in 30 seconds.

3 Meanwhile, mix the potato flour with the salt in a bowl. Lift the chicken out of the marinade and shake off any excess. Drop it into the potato flour and coat well, then shake off any excess.

4 Add the chicken to the oil, in batches, and cook for 6 minutes, or until crisp and brown. Remove, drain on kitchen paper and keep hot while you cook the remaining chicken.

5 Serve with lemon wedges.

beef stir-fry

ingredients

SERVES 4

2 tbsp vegetable or peanut oil

2 medium red onions, sliced
thinly

2 garlic cloves, chopped

2.5-cm/1-inch piece ginger,
cut into thin sticks

2 x 115-g/4-oz beef fillets,
sliced thinly

1 green pepper, deseeded
and sliced

150 g/5^1/$_2$ oz canned
bamboo shoots

115 g/4 oz bean sprouts

2 tbsp Thai magic paste
(see below)

1 tbsp Thai red curry paste

handful of fresh coriander,
chopped

few sprigs Thai basil

boiled rice, to serve

thai magic paste

whole bulb of garlic, peeled

bunch of fresh coriander
leaves and roots,
roughly chopped

55 g/2 oz white peppercorns

method

1 To make the Thai magic paste, pulse all the ingredients briefly in a blender or food processor to form a thick paste, or pound with a pestle until well mixed. Store in the refrigerator for 3–4 days or freeze in small amounts.

2 Heat the oil in a wok and stir-fry the onions, garlic and root ginger for 1 minute.

3 Add the beef strips and stir-fry over high heat until browned all over.

4 Add the vegetables and the magic and curry pastes and cook for 2–3 minutes until blended and cooked.

5 Stir in the coriander and basil and serve immediately with rice.

crispy pork dumplings

ingredients

SERVES 4

350 g/12 oz ground pork

2 tbsp finely chopped fresh
coriander

1 garlic clove, crushed

1 fresh green chilli, deseeded
and chopped

3 tbsp cornflour

1 egg white

1/2 tsp salt

16 wonton skins

1 tbsp water

vegetable or peanut oil,
for cooking

chilli sauce, to serve

method

1 Put the pork in a bowl and beat in the coriander, garlic, chilli, 1 tablespoon of the cornflour, the egg white and salt. Beat together to a thick, smooth texture. With damp hands shape into 16 equal portions and roll into balls.

2 Put a pork ball in the centre of each wonton skin. Make a paste by mixing the remaining cornflour with 1 tablespoon of water. Brush the edges of the skins with the cornflour paste and gather them up around the filling to make half into small, sacklike parcels, and the rest into triangular shapes.

3 Arrange the dumplings in a single layer (in batches if need be) in the top of a steamer and cook over boiling water for 10–15 minutes, until the meat is cooked through.

4 Heat the oil in a wok and carefully drop the parcels into it. Deep-fry for 2–3 minutes, until golden brown and crisp. Drain on kitchen paper.

5 Serve hot with chilli sauce.

soft-wrapped pork & prawn rolls

ingredients

MAKES 20 PIECES

115 g/4 oz firm tofu

3 tbsp vegetable or peanut oil

1 tsp finely chopped garlic

55 g/2 oz lean pork, shredded

115 g/4 oz raw prawns,
   peeled and deveined

1/2 small carrot, cut into short
   thin sticks

55 g/2 oz fresh or canned
   bamboo shoots, rinsed
   and shredded (if using
   fresh shoots, boil in water
   first for 30 minutes)

115 g/4 oz very finely sliced
   cabbage

55 g/2 oz mangetout,
   julienned

1-egg omelette, shredded

1 tsp salt

1 tsp light soy sauce

1 tsp Shaoxing rice wine

pinch of white pepper

20 soft spring roll skins

chilli bean sauce, to serve

method

1 Slice the tofu into thin slices horizontally and cook in 1 tablespoon of the oil until it turns golden brown. Cut into thin strips and set aside.

2 In a preheated wok, heat the remaining oil and stir-fry the garlic until fragrant. Add the pork and stir for about 1 minute, then add the prawns and stir for a further minute.

3 One by one, stirring well after each addition, add the carrot, bamboo shoots, cabbage, mangetout, tofu and, finally, the shredded omelette.

4 Season with the salt, light soy sauce, Shaoxing rice wine and pepper. Stir for a further minute, then turn out into a serving dish.

5 To assemble each roll, smear a skin with a little chilli bean sauce and place a heaped teaspoon of the filling towards the bottom of the circle. Roll up the bottom edge to secure the filling, turn in the sides, and continue to roll up gently. Serve with chilli bean sauce on the side.

spring rolls

ingredients

MAKES 20–25 PIECES

6 dried Chinese mushrooms,
    soaked in warm water
    for 20 minutes
1 tbsp vegetable or peanut oil
225 g/8 oz minced pork
1 tsp dark soy sauce
100 g/3^1/$_2$ oz fresh or canned
    bamboo shoots, rinsed
    and julienned (if using
    fresh shoots, boil in water
    first for 30 minutes)
pinch of salt
100 g/3^1/$_2$ oz raw prawns,
    peeled, deveined and
    chopped
225 g/8 oz bean sprouts,
    trimmed and roughly
    chopped
1 tbsp finely chopped spring
    onions
25 spring roll skins
1 egg white, lightly beaten
vegetable or peanut oil,
    for deep-frying

method

1 Squeeze out any excess water from the mushrooms and finely slice, discarding any tough stems.

2 In a preheated wok, heat the tablespoon of oil and stir-fry the pork until it changes colour. Add the dark soy sauce, bamboo shoots, mushrooms and a little salt. Stir over high heat for 3 minutes.

3 Add the prawns and cook for 2 minutes, then add the bean sprouts and cook for a further minute. Remove from the heat and stir in the spring onion. Set aside to cool.

4 Place a tablespoon of the mixture towards the bottom of a skin. Roll once to secure the filling, then fold in the sides to create a 10-cm/4-inch piece and continue to roll up. Seal with egg white.

5 Heat enough oil for deep-frying in a wok or deep-fat fryer until it reaches 180–190°C/350–375°F, or until a cube of bread browns in 30 seconds. Without overcrowding the wok, fry the rolls for about 5 minutes until golden brown and crispy.

crispy wrapped prawns

ingredients

SERVES 4

16 large, unpeeled cooked
    prawns

juice of 1 lime

4 tbsp chilli sauce

16 wonton skins

vegetable or peanut oil,
    for deep-frying

plum sauce, to serve

method

1 Remove the heads and shell the prawns, but leave the tails intact. Place them in a non-metallic bowl, add the lime juice and toss lightly to coat. Set aside in a cool place for 30 minutes.

2 Spread a little chilli sauce over a wonton skin. Place a prawn diagonally across it, leaving the tail protruding. Fold the bottom corner of the skin over the prawn, fold the next corner up over the head, and then roll the prawn up in the skin so that the body is encased, but the tail is exposed. Repeat with the remaining skins, chilli sauce and prawns.

3 Heat the oil in a wok and deep-fry the prawns, in batches, until crisp and browned. Serve hot with plum sauce for dipping.

prawn toasts

ingredients

MAKES 16 PIECES

100 g/3¹/₂ oz raw prawns,
    peeled and deveined
2 egg whites
2 tbsp cornflour
¹/₂ tsp sugar
pinch of salt
2 tbsp finely chopped
    coriander leaves
2 slices day-old white bread
vegetable or peanut oil, for
    deep-frying

method

1 Pound the prawns to a pulp in a pestle and mortar or with the base of a cleaver.

2 Mix the prawns with one of the egg whites and 1 tablespoon of the cornflour. Add the sugar and salt and stir in the chopped coriander. Mix the remaining egg white with the remaining cornflour.

3 Remove the crusts from the bread and cut each slice into 8 triangles. Brush the top of each piece with the egg white and cornflour mixture, then add 1 teaspoon of the prawn mixture. Smooth the top.

4 Heat enough oil for deep-frying in a wok until it reaches 180–190°C/350–375°F, or until a cube of bread browns in 30 seconds. Without overcrowding the wok, cook the toasts prawn-side up for about 2 minutes. Turn and cook for a further 2 minutes, or until beginning to turn golden brown.

5 Drain and serve warm.

crisp sesame prawns

ingredients

SERVES 4

115 g/4 oz self-raising flour

3 tbsp sesame seeds, toasted
   or dry-fried

1 tsp Thai red curry paste

1 tbsp fish sauce

150 ml/5 fl oz water

vegetable or peanut oil, for
   deep-frying

20 large, uncooked prawns,
   peeled with tails intact

chilli sauce, for dipping

method

1 Combine the flour and sesame seeds in a bowl. Stir the curry paste, fish sauce and water together in a jug until mixed. Gradually pour the liquid into the flour, stirring constantly, to make a thick batter.

2 Heat the oil for deep-frying in a wok. Holding the prawns by their tails, dip them into the batter, one at a time, then carefully drop into the hot oil. Cook for 2–3 minutes, until crisp and brown. Drain on kitchen paper.

3 Serve immediately with chilli sauce.

crab parcels

ingredients

SERVES 4

350 g/12 oz canned white
     crabmeat, drained

1 fresh red chilli, deseeded
     and chopped

4 spring onions, sliced finely

1 tbsp Thai red curry paste

juice of $1/2$ lime

$1/2$ tsp salt

20 wonton skins

oil for cooking

dip

55 g/2 oz caster sugar

2 tbsp water

2 tbsp rice wine vinegar

3 pieces preserved ginger,
     sliced

1 tbsp ginger syrup from the jar

method

1 Put the crabmeat into a bowl and add the chilli, spring onions and curry paste. Stir together with the lime juice and salt.

2 Put the skins in a pile and put 1 portion of the crabmeat in the centre of the top skin. Brush the edges with a little water and roll up the edges to make a small cigar-shaped parcel. Continue to make parcels with the skins – you need at least 20.

3 Heat the oil in a wok and cook the parcels, a few at a time, until golden brown. Drain on kitchen paper.

4 Put all the ingredients for the dip in a small pan and heat gently until the sugar has melted. Serve warm with the crab parcels.

vegetarian spring rolls

ingredients

MAKES 18–20 PIECES

6 dried Chinese mushrooms, soaked in warm water for 20 minutes

55 g/2 oz beanthread noodles, soaked in warm water for 20 minutes

2 tbsp vegetable or peanut oil

1 tbsp finely chopped fresh root ginger

100 g/3^1/2 oz carrot, julienned

100 g/3^1/2 oz finely shredded cabbage

1 tbsp finely sliced spring onion

1 tbsp light soy sauce

85 g/3 oz soft tofu, cut into small cubes

^{1}/2 tsp salt

pinch of white pepper

pinch of sugar

20 spring roll skins

1 egg white, lightly beaten

vegetable or peanut oil, for deep-frying

soy sauce, for dipping

method

1 Squeeze out any excess water from the mushrooms and finely chop, discarding any tough stems. Drain the beanthread noodles and roughly chop.

2 In a preheated wok, heat the oil, then toss in the ginger and cook until fragrant. Add the mushrooms and stir for about 2 minutes. Add the carrot, cabbage and spring onion and stir-fry for 1 minute. Add the beanthread noodles and light soy sauce and stir-fry for 1 minute. Add the tofu and cook for a further minute. Season with the salt, pepper and sugar and mix well. Continue cooking for 1–2 minutes, or until the carrot is soft. Remove from the heat and set aside to cool.

3 Place a scant tablespoon of the mixture towards the bottom of a skin. Roll once to secure the filling, then fold in the sides to create a 10-cm/4-inch piece and continue to roll up. Seal with egg white.

4 Heat enough oil for deep-frying in a wok or deep-fat fryer until it reaches 180–190°C/350–375°F, or until a cube of bread browns in 30 seconds. Without overcrowding the wok, cook the rolls for about 5 minutes, or until golden brown and crispy.

5 Serve with a good soy sauce for dipping.

vegetable parcels

ingredients

SERVES 4

2 tbsp vegetable or peanut oil

225 g/8 oz potatoes, diced
    and boiled for 5 minutes

2 garlic cloves, crushed

1 onion, chopped

2 tbsp Thai green curry paste

55 g/2 oz frozen peas, thawed

juice of 1 lime

$1/2$ tsp salt

16 x 10-cm/4-inch square
    egg roll skins

1 egg, beaten

vegetable or peanut oil, for
    deep-frying

sweet chilli sauce or Thai soy
    sauce, to serve

method

1 Heat the oil in a wok and stir-fry the potatoes, garlic, onion and curry paste until lightly browned. Stir in the peas, lime juice, and salt and stir-fry for 1–2 minutes. Remove from the heat.

2 Brush 1 egg roll skin with egg. Put a small spoonful of the potato mixture in the centre and fold up the edges to enclose the filling and make a purse-shaped parcel. Press the skin tightly together to seal the parcel. Repeat with the remaining skins and filling to make 16 small parcels.

3 Heat the oil for deep-frying in a wok. Add the vegetable parcels, in batches, and deep-fry for 3–4 minutes, until golden brown. Drain on kitchen paper and keep warm while you cook the remaining parcels.

4 Serve hot with a bowl of chilli sauce or soy sauce for dipping.

wontons

ingredients

SERVES 4

filling

2 tbsp vegetable or peanut oil

6 spring onions, chopped

125 g/4$^{1}/_{2}$ oz mushrooms, chopped

55 g/2 oz fine green beans, chopped

55 g/2 oz sweetcorn kernels, drained if canned

1 egg, beaten

3 tbsp Thai soy sauce

1 tbsp jaggery or soft light brown sugar

$^{1}/_{2}$ tsp salt

wontons

24 wonton skins

1 egg, beaten

vegetable or peanut oil, for deep-frying

plum or chilli sauce, to serve

method

1 To make the filling, heat the oil in a preheated wok and stir-fry the spring onions, mushrooms and beans for 1–2 minutes, until softened. Add the sweetcorn, stir well to mix and then push the vegetables to the side.

2 Pour in the egg. Stir until lightly set before incorporating the vegetables and adding the soy sauce, sugar and salt. Remove the wok from the heat.

3 Place the wonton skins in a pile on a work surface. Put a teaspoonful of the filling in the centre of the top skin. Brush the edges with beaten egg and fold in half diagonally to make a small triangular parcel. Repeat with the remaining skins and filling.

4 Heat the oil for deep-frying in a wok. Add the parcels, in batches, and deep-fry for 3–4 minutes, until golden brown. Remove from the wok with a slotted spoon and drain on kitchen paper. Keep warm while you cook the remaining wontons.

5 Serve hot with plum or chilli sauce.

crispy seaweed

ingredients

SERVES 4

1 kg/2 lb 4 oz pak choi
850 ml/1 1/2 pints peanut oil
1 tsp salt
1 tbsp caster sugar
85 g/3 oz toasted pine nuts

method

1 Rinse the pak choi leaves under cold running water, then pat dry thoroughly with kitchen paper.

2 Discarding any tough outer leaves, roll each pak choi leaf up, then slice thinly so that the leaves are finely shredded. Alternatively, use a food processor to shred the pak choi.

3 Heat the peanut oil in a large preheated wok. Carefully add the shredded pak choi and cook for 30 seconds, or until it shrivels up and becomes crispy. (You will probably need to do this in several batches.) Remove from the wok with a slotted spoon and drain thoroughly on kitchen paper.

4 Transfer to a large bowl, toss with the salt, sugar and toasted pine nuts, and serve.

tempura

ingredients

SERVES 4

150 g/5¹/₂ oz packet
    tempura mix
4 shiitake mushrooms
4 fresh asparagus spears
4 slices sweet potato
1 red pepper, deseeded and
    cut into strips
4 onion slices, cut widthways
    into rings
oil, for deep-frying

dipping sauce

2 tsp mirin
1 tbsp shoyu (Japanese
    soy sauce)
pinch of dashi granules,
    dissolved in 2 tbsp
    boiling water

method

1 To make the dipping sauce, mix the ingredients together in a small dipping dish.

2 Mix the tempura with water according to the packet instructions. Don't try to make the batter smooth – it should be a little lumpy. Drop the vegetables into the batter.

3 Preheat a wok, then fill two-thirds full with oil, or use a deep-fryer. Heat the oil to 180–190°C/350–375°F, or until a cube of bread browns in 30 seconds.

4 Lift 2–3 pieces of tempura out of the batter, add to the oil and cook for 2–3 minutes, or until the batter is a light golden colour. Remove, drain on kitchen paper and keep hot while you cook the remaining tempura pieces.

5 Serve with the dipping sauce.

meat & poultry

Stir-frying is a fast and very efficient way to cook meat and poultry, because the meat is cut into thin strips or small cubes, needing only minutes to cook through. Check your recipe carefully, though, because some dishes require the meat to stand in a marinade for some hours before cooking! Spicy Beef with Potato is an excellent example – the meat bathes overnight in a paste of soy and fish sauces, herbs, garlic and peppercorns, but the following day you will need less than 30 minutes to produce a one-pot (or, in this case, one-wok!) meal of tender beef, potatoes and spinach.

The Thai people often use their woks for cooking curries. Thai curry paste comes in several varieties, including red, green and yellow, which are readily available in jars. Make sure you use the right colour for the recipe, because there is a difference – green is very hot, red is a little less fiery and yellow is the mildest. Chinese marinades and sauces are lighter and more delicate in flavour, often with a sweet-and-sour taste contrast, while thicker sauces tend to be based on beans.

If you don't yet own a wok, you can use a deep, heavy-based pan instead, but the point of the wok is that the shape ensures an even distribution of heat, reducing the cooking time and ensuring that the nutritional value of the ingredients is retained.

mussaman curry

ingredients

SERVES 4

1 tbsp vegetable or peanut oil

450 g/1 lb beef topside,
    cut into cubes

2 tbsp Mussaman curry paste

2 large onions, cut into
    wedges

2 large potatoes, cut into
    chunks

400 ml/14 fl oz coconut milk

150 ml/5 fl oz water

2 cardamom pods

2 tbsp tamarind paste

2 tsp jaggery or soft light
    brown sugar

75 g/2¾ oz unsalted
    peanuts, toasted or
    dry-fried

1 fresh red chilli, sliced thinly

boiled rice, to serve

method

1 Heat the oil in a wok and cook the meat, in batches, until browned all over. Remove with a slotted spoon and set aside.

2 Add the curry paste to the wok and stir-fry for 1–2 minutes. Add the onions and potatoes and stir-fry for 4–5 minutes, until golden brown. Remove with a slotted spoon and set aside.

3 Pour the coconut milk into the wok with the measured water and bring to the boil. Reduce the heat and simmer for 8–10 minutes.

4 Return the meat and cooked vegetables to the wok. Add the cardamom, tamarind paste and sugar and simmer for 15–20 minutes, until the meat is tender. Stir in the peanuts and chilli and serve with rice.

spicy beef with potato

ingredients

SERVES 4

450 g/1 lb beef fillet

2 tbsp Thai soy sauce

2 tbsp fish sauce

2 tbsp vegetable or peanut oil

3–4 coriander roots, chopped

1 tbsp crushed black
    peppercorns

2 garlic cloves, chopped

1 tbsp jaggery or soft light
    brown sugar

350 g/12 oz potatoes, diced

150 ml/5 fl oz water

bunch of spring onions,
    chopped

225 g/8 oz baby spinach
    leaves

cooked rice or noodles, to serve

method

1 Cut the beef into thick slices and place in
a shallow dish. Put the soy sauce, fish sauce,
1 tablespoon of the oil, the coriander roots,
peppercorns, garlic and sugar in a food
processor and process to a thick paste. Scrape
the paste into the dish and toss the beef to coat.
Cover with clingfilm and set aside to marinate
in the refrigerator for at least 3 hours, and
preferably overnight.

2 Heat the remaining oil in a wok. Lift the beef
out of the marinade, reserving the marinade,
and cook for 3–4 minutes on each side, until
browned. Add the reserved marinade and the
potatoes with the measured water and gradually
bring to the boil. Simmer for 6–8 minutes, or
until the potatoes are tender.

3 Add the spring onions and spinach. Cook
gently until the greens have wilted. Serve
immediately with rice or noodles.

beef chop suey

ingredients

SERVES 4

450 g/1 lb ribeye or sirloin
    steak, finely sliced

1 head of broccoli, cut into
    small florets

2 tbsp vegetable or peanut oil

1 onion, finely sliced

2 celery stalks, finely sliced
    diagonally

225 g/8 oz mangetout, sliced
    in half lengthways

55 g/2 oz fresh or canned
    bamboo shoots, rinsed
    and julienned (if using
    fresh shoots, boil in water
    first for 30 minutes)

8 water chestnuts, finely sliced

225 g/8 oz finely sliced
    mushrooms

1 tbsp oyster sauce

1 tsp salt

freshly cooked rice, to serve

marinade

1 tbsp Shaoxing rice wine

pinch of white pepper

pinch of salt

1 tbsp light soy sauce

$^1/_2$ tsp sesame oil

method

1 Combine all the marinade ingredients
in a bowl and marinate the beef for at least
20 minutes. Blanch the broccoli in a large
pan of boiling water for 30 seconds. Drain
and set aside.

2 In a preheated wok, heat 1 tablespoon of
the oil and stir-fry the beef until the colour has
changed. Remove and set aside.

3 In the clean wok, heat the remaining oil and
stir-fry the onion for 1 minute. Add the celery
and broccoli and cook for 2 minutes. Add the
mangetout, bamboo shoots, chestnuts and
mushrooms and cook for 1 minute. Add the
beef, then season with the oyster sauce and
salt and serve with freshly cooked rice.

beef with onions & broccoli

ingredients

SERVES 4

2 tbsp vegetable or peanut oil

2 tbsp Thai green curry paste

2 x 175-g/6-oz sirloin steaks,
    sliced thinly

2 onions, sliced

6 spring onions, chopped

2 shallots, chopped finely

225 g/8 oz head of broccoli,
    cut into florets

400 ml/14 fl oz coconut milk

3 kaffir lime leaves, chopped
    roughly

4 tbsp chopped fresh
    coriander

few Thai basil leaves

method

1 Heat the oil in a wok and stir-fry the curry paste for 1–2 minutes. Add the meat, in batches if necessary, and stir-fry until starting to brown.

2 Add the onions, spring onions and shallots, and stir-fry for 2–3 minutes. Add the broccoli and stir-fry for 2–3 minutes.

3 Pour in the coconut milk, add the lime leaves and bring to the boil. Simmer gently for 8–10 minutes, until the meat is tender. Stir in the coriander and basil and serve immediately.

stir-fried beef with broccoli & ginger

ingredients

SERVES 4–6

350 g/12 oz tenderloin steak,
    cut into thin strips

175 g/6 oz broccoli florets

2 tbsp vegetable or peanut oil

1 garlic clove, finely chopped

1 tsp finely chopped fresh
    root ginger

1 small onion, finely sliced

1 tsp salt

1 tsp light soy sauce

marinade

1 tbsp light soy sauce

1 tsp sesame oil

1 tsp Shaoxing rice wine

1 tsp sugar

pinch of white pepper

method

1 Combine the marinade ingredients in a bowl, then mix in the beef. Cover and stand for 1 hour, basting occasionally. Blanch the broccoli in a large pan of boiling water for 30 seconds. Drain and set aside.

2 In a preheated wok, heat 1 tablespoon of the oil and stir-fry the garlic, root ginger and onion for 1 minute. Add the broccoli and stir-fry for a further minute. Remove from the wok and set aside.

3 In the clean preheated wok, heat the remaining oil and stir-fry the beef until the colour has changed. Return the broccoli mixture to the wok with the salt and light soy sauce and stir until cooked through. Serve immediately.

hot sesame beef

ingredients

SERVES 4

500 g/1 lb 2 oz beef fillet,
    cut into thin strips

1¹/₂ tbsp sesame seeds

125 ml/4 fl oz beef stock

2 tbsp soy sauce

2 tbsp grated fresh root ginger

2 garlic cloves, chopped finely

1 tsp cornflour

¹/₂ tsp chilli flakes

3 tbsp sesame oil

1 large head of broccoli,
    cut into florets

1 orange pepper, sliced thinly

1 red chilli, deseeded and
    sliced finely

1 tbsp chilli oil (optional)

cooked long-grain and wild
    rice, to serve

1 tbsp chopped fresh
    coriander, to garnish

method

1 Mix the beef strips with 1 tablespoon of the sesame seeds in a small bowl. In a separate bowl, whisk together the beef stock, soy sauce, root ginger, garlic, cornflour and chilli flakes.

2 Heat 1 tablespoon of the sesame oil in a wok. Stir-fry the beef strips for 2–3 minutes. Remove and set aside.

3 Discard any oil remaining in the wok, then wipe with kitchen paper to remove any stray sesame seeds. Heat the remaining oil and add the broccoli, orange pepper, chilli and chilli oil (if desired), then stir-fry for 2–3 minutes. Stir in the beef bouillon mixture, then cover and simmer for 2 minutes.

4 Return the beef to the wok and simmer until the juices thicken, stirring occasionally. Cook for another 1–2 minutes.

5 Sprinkle with the remaining sesame seeds. Serve over cooked long-grain and wild rice and garnish with fresh coriander.

ma po doufu

ingredients

SERVES 4

450 g/1 lb tofu

2 tbsp vegetable or peanut oil

1 tsp Sichuan peppers

100 g/3^1/$_2$ oz minced beef

2 tbsp chilli bean sauce

1 tsp fermented black beans,
    rinsed and lightly mashed

100 ml/3^1/$_2$ fl oz
    hot chicken stock

pinch of sugar

1 tsp light soy sauce

pinch of salt

2 tbsp thinly sliced spring
    onion, cut on the diagonal

method

1 Cut the tofu into 2-cm/^{3}/4-inch cubes and arrange in a large pan. Pour over enough boiling water to cover and set aside.

2 In a preheated wok, heat the oil until almost smoking. Throw in the Sichuan peppers and stir until fragrant. Add the beef and stir-fry until brown and crispy.

3 Lower the heat and add the chilli bean sauce and black beans and stir for about 30 seconds, or until the oil is richly red.

4 Pour in the hot chicken stock and gently add the drained tofu. Season with the sugar, light soy sauce and salt. Simmer for about 5 minutes.

5 Finally, toss in the spring onion. Transfer into 1 large or 4 individual bowls and serve.

katsudon

ingredients

SERVES 4

4 tbsp plain flour

1 egg, lightly beaten

115 g/4 oz Tonkatsu (panko)
    breadcrumbs

4 pork chops, about 150 g/
    5$^1/_2$ oz each, bones
    removed

oil, for pan-frying

600 ml/1 pint dashi stock

4 tbsp shoyu (Japanese
    soy sauce)

2 tbsp mirin

1 onion, sliced

4 eggs

600 g/1 lb 5 oz cooked
    Japanese short-grain rice

method

1 Put the flour, egg and breadcrumbs separately into 3 shallow bowls large enough to fit a pork chop. Roll a rolling pin over each chop to thin it a little.

2 Dip each chop first in the flour, then in the egg and finally in the breadcrumbs to coat. Cover with clingfilm and chill in the refrigerator for 10 minutes, then dip again in the egg and the breadcrumbs.

3 Preheat a wok over high heat. Add oil to a depth of about 2 cm/3/4 inch and heat until very hot. Add the chops, one at a time, reduce the heat to medium and cook for 4 minutes on each side, or until the pork is cooked through and the breadcrumbs are golden. Remove and slice.

4 Meanwhile, put the stock, soy sauce and mirin in a pan and bring to a simmer. Add the onion and simmer for 5 minutes. Beat the eggs in a bowl, then pour over the onions in the stock. Cover and cook for 1 minute.

5 Divide the rice between 4 bowls. Lay the pork slices on top, then ladle some of the egg, onion and stock over the pork and rice. Serve immediately.

spicy sichuan pork

ingredients

SERVES 4

280 g/10 oz pork belly, thinly
    sliced
1 tbsp vegetable or peanut oil
1 tbsp chilli bean sauce
1 tbsp fermented black beans,
    rinsed and lightly mashed
1 tsp sweet red bean paste
    (optional)
1 green pepper, finely sliced
1 red pepper, finely sliced
1 tsp sugar
1 tsp dark soy sauce
pinch of white pepper

freshly cooked rice, to serve

method

1 If cooking the pork especially for this dish,
bring a pan of water to the boil and place the
pork in the pan, then cover and simmer for
about 20 minutes, skimming occasionally. Let
the pork cool and rest before slicing thinly.

2 In a preheated wok, heat the oil and stir-fry
the pork slices until they begin to shrink. Stir
in the chilli bean sauce, then add the black
beans and the red bean paste, if using.
Finally, toss in the peppers and the remaining
ingredients and stir-fry for 2 minutes. Serve
with freshly cooked rice.

hoisin pork with garlic noodles

ingredients

SERVES 4

250 g/9 oz dried thick Chinese
   egg noodles, or Chinese
   wholemeal egg noodles

450 g/1 lb pork fillet,
   thinly sliced

1 tsp sugar

1 tbsp peanut or corn oil

4 tbsp rice vinegar

4 tbsp white wine vinegar

4 tbsp bottled hoisin sauce

2 spring onions, sliced on
   the diagonal

about 2 tbsp garlic-flavoured
   corn oil

2 large garlic cloves, thinly
   sliced

chopped fresh coriander,
   to garnish

method

1 Start by boiling the noodles for 3 minutes, until soft. Alternatively, cook according to the packet instructions. Drain well, rinse under cold water to stop the cooking and drain again, then set aside.

2 Meanwhile, sprinkle the pork slices with the sugar and use your hands to toss together. Heat a wok over high heat. Add the oil and heat until it shimmers. Add the pork and stir-fry for about 3 minutes, until the pork is cooked through and is no longer pink. Use a slotted spoon to remove the pork from the wok and keep warm. Add both vinegars to the wok and boil until they are reduced to about 5 tablespoons. Pour in the hoisin sauce with the spring onions and let it bubble until reduced by half. Add to the pork and stir together.

3 Quickly wipe out the wok and reheat. Add the garlic-flavoured oil and heat until it shimmers. Add the garlic slices and stir round for about 30 seconds, until they are golden and crisp, then use a slotted spoon to scoop them out of the wok and set aside.

4 Add the noodles to the wok and stir them round to warm them through. Divide the noodles between 4 plates, top with the pork and onion mixture and sprinkle over the garlic slices and coriander.

pork & crab meatballs

ingredients

SERVES 6

225 g/8 oz pork fillet,
    chopped finely
170 g/5³/4 oz canned
    crabmeat, drained
3 spring onions, chopped
    finely
1 garlic clove, chopped finely
1 tsp Thai red curry paste
1 tbsp cornflour
1 egg white
vegetable or peanut oil,
    for deep-frying
boiled rice, to serve

sauce

1 tbsp vegetable or peanut oil
2 shallots, chopped
1 garlic clove, crushed
2 large fresh red chillies,
    deseeded and chopped
4 spring onions, chopped
3 tomatoes, chopped roughly

method

1 Put the pork and crabmeat into a bowl and mix together. Add the spring onions, garlic, curry paste, cornflour and egg white and beat together well to make a thick paste. With damp hands shape the mixture into walnut-size balls.

2 Heat the oil in a wok and deep-fry the balls, in batches, for 3–4 minutes, turning frequently, until golden brown and cooked. Drain on kitchen paper and keep warm.

3 To make the sauce, heat the oil in a wok and stir-fry the shallots and garlic for 1–2 minutes. Add the chillies and spring onions and stir-fry for 1–2 minutes, then add the tomatoes. Stir together quickly, then spoon the sauce over the pork and crab balls. Serve immediately with rice.

pork with peppers

ingredients

SERVES 4

1 tbsp vegetable or peanut oil

1 tbsp chilli oil

450 g/1 lb pork fillet, sliced
 thinly

2 tbsp green chilli sauce

6 spring onions, sliced

2.5-cm/1-inch piece fresh
 root ginger, sliced thinly

1 red pepper, deseeded
 and sliced

1 yellow pepper, deseeded
 and sliced

1 orange pepper, deseeded
 and sliced

1 tbsp fish sauce

2 tbsp Thai soy sauce

juice of $1/2$ lime

4 tbsp chopped fresh parsley

cooked flat rice noodles,
 to serve

method

1 Heat both the oils in a wok. Add the pork, in batches, and stir-fry until browned all over. Remove with a slotted spoon and set aside.

2 Add the chilli sauce, spring onions and root ginger to the wok and stir-fry for 1–2 minutes. Add the peppers and stir-fry for 2–3 minutes.

3 Return the meat to the wok, stir well and add the fish sauce, soy sauce and lime juice. Cook for a further 1–2 minutes, then stir in the parsley and serve with flat rice noodles.

spareribs in a sweet-&-sour sauce

ingredients

SERVES 4

450 g/1 lb spareribs, cut into
bite-size pieces (you or
your butcher can cut ribs
into pieces with a cleaver)
vegetable or peanut oil,
for deep-frying

marinade

2 tsp light soy sauce
$^1/_2$ tsp salt
pinch of white pepper

sauce

3 tbsp white rice vinegar
2 tbsp sugar
1 tbsp light soy sauce
1 tbsp tomato ketchup
$1^1/_2$ tbsp vegetable or peanut oil
1 green pepper, roughly
chopped
1 small onion, roughly chopped
1 small carrot, finely sliced
$^1/_2$ tsp finely chopped garlic
$^1/_2$ tsp finely chopped root
ginger
100 g/$3^1/_2$ oz pineapple
chunks

method

1 Combine the marinade ingredients in a bowl with the pork and marinate for at least 20 minutes.

2 Heat enough oil for deep-frying in a wok or deep-fat fryer until it reaches 180–190°C/350–375°F, or until a cube of bread browns in 30 seconds. Deep-fry the spareribs for 8 minutes. Drain and set aside.

3 To prepare the sauce, first mix together the vinegar, sugar, light soy sauce and ketchup. Set aside.

4 In a preheated wok, heat 1 tablespoon of the oil and stir-fry the pepper, onion and carrot for 2 minutes. Remove and set aside.

5 In the clean preheated wok, heat the remaining oil and stir-fry the garlic and root ginger until fragrant. Add the vinegar mixture. Bring back to the boil and add the pineapple chunks. Finally add the spareribs and the pepper, onion and carrot. Stir until warmed through and serve immediately.

chicken with cashew nuts

ingredients

SERVES 4–6

450 g/1 lb boneless chicken
    meat, cut into bite-size
    pieces

3 tbsp light soy sauce

1 tsp Shaoxing rice wine

pinch of sugar

1/2 tsp salt

3 dried Chinese mushrooms,
    soaked in warm water for
    20 minutes

2 tbsp vegetable or peanut oil

4 slices of fresh root ginger

1 tsp finely chopped garlic

1 red pepper, cut into
    2.5-cm/1-inch squares

85 g/3 oz cashew nuts,
    roasted

method

1 Marinate the chicken in 2 tablespoons of the light soy sauce, Shaoxing, sugar and salt for at least 20 minutes.

2 Squeeze any excess water from the mushrooms and slice finely, discarding any tough stems. Reserve the soaking water.

3 In a preheated wok, heat 1 tablespoon of the oil. Add the root ginger and stir-fry until fragrant. Stir in the chicken and cook for 2 minutes, or until it begins to turn brown. Before the chicken is cooked through, remove and set aside.

4 In the clean wok, heat the remaining oil and stir-fry the garlic until fragrant. Add the mushrooms and red pepper and stir-fry for 1 minute. Add about 2 tablespoons of the mushroom soaking water and cook for about 2 minutes, or until the water has evaporated.

5 Return the chicken to the wok, then add the remaining light soy sauce and the cashew nuts and stir-fry for 2 minutes, or until the chicken is cooked through.

san choy bau

ingredients

MAKES 6

1 tbsp vegetable or peanut oil

100 g/3^1/$_2$ oz chicken, finely
    chopped

25 g/1 oz water chestnuts,
    finely chopped

1 tsp finely chopped Chinese
    chives

25 g/1 oz pine nuts,
    lightly toasted

1 tsp salt

^{1}/$_2$ tsp white pepper

6 lettuce leaves, washed

3 tsp plum sauce, to serve

method

1 In a preheated wok, heat the oil and stir-fry the chicken for 1 minute. Add the water chestnuts and chives and cook for 2 minutes. Add the pine nuts and cook for 1 minute. Add the salt and pepper and stir.

2 To serve, place a spoonful in the centre of each lettuce leaf, then top with the plum sauce and fold the lettuce leaf to make a small roll.

sweet-&-sour chicken

ingredients

SERVES 4–6

450 g/1 lb lean chicken meat, cubed

5 tbsp vegetable or peanut oil

1/2 tsp crushed garlic

1/2 tsp finely chopped fresh root ginger

1 green pepper, roughly chopped

1 onion, roughly chopped

1 carrot, finely sliced

1 tsp sesame oil

1 tbsp finely chopped spring onion

marinade

2 tsp light soy sauce

1 tsp Shaoxing rice wine

pinch of white pepper

1/2 tsp salt

dash of sesame oil

sauce

8 tbsp rice vinegar

4 tbsp sugar

2 tsp light soy sauce

6 tbsp tomato ketchup

method

1 Place all the marinade ingredients in a bowl and marinate the chicken pieces for at least 20 minutes.

2 To prepare the sauce, heat the vinegar in a pan and add the sugar, light soy sauce and tomato ketchup. Stir to dissolve the sugar, then set aside.

3 In a preheated wok, heat 3 tablespoons of the oil and stir-fry the chicken until it starts to turn golden brown. Remove and set aside.

4 In the clean wok, heat the remaining oil and cook the garlic and root ginger until fragrant. Add the vegetables and cook for 2 minutes. Add the chicken and cook for 1 minute. Finally add the sauce and sesame oil, then stir in the spring onion and serve.

gong bau chicken

ingredients

SERVES 4

2 boneless chicken breasts,
   with or without skin, cut
   into 1-cm/^{1}/$_2$-inch cubes

1 tbsp vegetable or peanut oil

10 dried red chillies or more,
   to taste, snipped into
   2 or 3 pieces

1 tsp Sichuan peppers

3 garlic cloves, finely sliced

2.5-cm/1-inch piece of fresh
   root ginger, finely sliced

1 tbsp roughly chopped
   spring onion, white
   part only

85 g/3 oz peanuts, roasted

marinade

2 tsp light soy sauce

1 tsp Shaoxing rice wine

^{1}/$_2$ tsp sugar

sauce

1 tsp light soy sauce

1 tsp dark soy sauce

1 tsp black Chinese rice vinegar

a few drops of sesame oil

2 tbsp chicken stock

1 tsp sugar

method

1 Combine all the ingredients for the marinade in a bowl and marinate the chicken, covered, for at least 20 minutes. Combine all the ingredients for the sauce and set aside.

2 In a preheated wok, heat the oil and stir-fry the chillies and peppers until crisp and fragrant. Toss in the chicken pieces. When they begin to turn white, add the garlic, root ginger and spring onion. Stir-fry for about 5 minutes, or until the chicken is cooked.

3 Pour in the sauce, mix together thoroughly, then stir in the peanuts. Serve immediately.

green chicken curry

ingredients

SERVES 4

1 tbsp vegetable or peanut oil

1 onion, sliced

1 garlic clove, chopped finely

2–3 tbsp Thai green
     curry paste

400 ml/14 fl oz coconut milk

150 ml/5 fl oz chicken stock

4 kaffir lime leaves

4 skinless, boneless chicken
     breasts, cut into cubes

1 tbsp fish sauce

2 tbsp Thai soy sauce

grated rind and juice of
     ¹/₂ lime

1 tsp jaggery or soft light
     brown sugar

4 tbsp chopped fresh
     coriander, to garnish

method

1 Heat the oil in a wok and stir-fry the onion
and garlic for 1–2 minutes, until starting to
soften. Add the curry paste and stir-fry for
1–2 minutes.

2 Add the coconut milk, stock and lime leaves,
bring to the boil and add the chicken. Reduce
the heat and simmer gently for 15–20 minutes,
until the chicken is tender.

3 Add the fish sauce, soy sauce, lime rind and
juice and sugar. Cook for 2–3 minutes, until
the sugar has dissolved. Serve immediately,
garnished with chopped coriander.

chicken with yellow curry sauce

ingredients

SERVES 4

spice paste

6 tbsp Thai yellow
curry paste
150 ml/5 fl oz plain yogurt
400 ml/14 fl oz water
handful of fresh coriander,
chopped
handful of fresh Thai basil
leaves, shredded

stir-fry

2 tbsp vegetable or peanut oil
2 onions, cut into thin wedges
2 garlic cloves, chopped finely
2 skinless, boneless chicken
breasts, cut into strips
175 g/6 oz baby corn cobs,
halved lengthways
chopped fresh coriander and
shredded fresh basil,
to garnish

method

1 To make the spice paste, stir-fry the yellow curry paste in a wok for 2–3 minutes, then stir in the yogurt, water and herbs. Bring to the boil, then simmer for 2–3 minutes.

2 Meanwhile, heat the oil in a wok and stir-fry the onions and garlic for 2–3 minutes. Add the chicken and baby corn cobs and stir-fry for 3–4 minutes, until the meat and corn are tender.

3 Stir in the spice paste and bring to the boil. Simmer for 2–3 minutes, until heated through. Serve immediately, garnished with extra herbs if desired.

gingered chicken & vegetable salad

ingredients

SERVES 4

4 skinless, boneless chicken
    breasts
4 spring onions, chopped
1.5-cm/1-inch piece fresh
    root ginger, chopped finely
2 garlic cloves, crushed
2 tbsp vegetable or peanut oil

salad

1 tbsp vegetable or peanut oil
1 onion, sliced
2 garlic cloves, chopped
115 g/4 oz baby corn cobs,
    halved
115 g/4 oz mangetout, halved
    lengthways
1 red pepper, deseeded
    and sliced
7.5-cm/3-inch piece
    cucumber, peeled,
    deseeded and sliced
4 tbsp Thai soy sauce
1 tbsp jaggery or soft light
    brown sugar
few Thai basil leaves
175 g/6 oz fine egg noodles

method

1 Cut the chicken into large cubes, each about 2.5 cm/1 inch. Mix the spring onions, root ginger, garlic and oil together in a shallow dish and add the chicken. Cover and marinate for at least 3 hours. Lift the meat out of the marinade and set aside.

2 Heat the oil in a wok and cook the onion for 1–2 minutes. Add the garlic and the rest of the vegetables, except the cucumber, and cook for 2–3 minutes, until just tender. Add the cucumber, half the soy sauce, the sugar and the basil, and mix gently.

3 Soak the noodles for 2–3 minutes (check the packet instructions) or until tender and drain well. Sprinkle the remaining soy sauce over them and arrange on plates. Top with the cooked vegetables.

4 Add a little more oil to the wok if necessary and cook the chicken over fairly high heat until browned on all sides. Arrange the chicken cubes on top of the salad and serve hot or warm.

red chicken salad

ingredients

SERVES 4

4 boneless chicken breasts

2 tbsp Thai red curry paste

2 tbsp vegetable or peanut oil

1 head Chinese leaves,
    shredded

175 g/6 oz pak choi, torn into
    large pieces

$1/2$ savoy cabbage, shredded

2 shallots, chopped finely

2 garlic cloves, crushed

1 tbsp rice wine vinegar

2 tbsp sweet chilli sauce

2 tbsp Thai soy sauce

method

1 Slash the flesh of the chicken several times and rub the curry paste into each cut. Cover and chill overnight.

2 Cook in a wok over medium heat for 5–6 minutes, turning once or twice, until cooked through. Keep warm.

3 Heat 1 tablespoon of the oil in a wok and stir-fry the pak choi and cabbage until just wilted. Add the remaining oil, shallots and garlic, and stir-fry until just tender but not browned. Add the vinegar, chilli sauce and soy. Remove from the heat.

4 Arrange the leaves on 4 serving plates. Slice the chicken, arrange on the salad leaves and drizzle the hot dressing over. Serve immediately.

turkey with bamboo shoots & water chestnuts

ingredients

SERVES 4

marinade

4 tbsp sweet sherry

1 tbsp lemon juice

1 tbsp soy sauce

2 tsp grated fresh root ginger

1 clove garlic, crushed

stir-fry

1 tbsp sesame oil

2 tbsp vegetable oil

450 g/1 lb turkey breast,
cubed

125 g/4^1/$_2$ oz small
mushrooms, cut
into halves

1 green pepper, cut
into strips

1 courgette, sliced thinly

4 spring onions, cut into
quarters

115 g/4 oz canned bamboo
shoots, drained

115 g/4 oz canned sliced
water chestnuts, drained

cooked noodles or rice, to
serve

method

1 Blend the sherry, lemon juice, soy sauce, root ginger and garlic in a bowl, then add the turkey and stir. Cover the dish with clingfilm and refrigerate to marinate for 3–4 hours.

2 In a wok, add the sesame oil and vegetable oil and heat slowly. Remove the turkey from the marinade with a slotted spoon (reserving the marinade) and stir-fry a few pieces at a time until browned. Remove the turkey from the wok and set aside.

3 Add the mushrooms, green pepper and courgette to the wok and stir-fry for 3 minutes. Add the spring onions and stir-fry for 1 minute more. Add the bamboo shoots and water chestnuts to the wok, then the turkey along with half of the reserved marinade. Stir over a medium-high heat for another 2–3 minutes, or until the ingredients are evenly coated and the marinade has reduced.

4 Serve immediately over noodles or rice.

duck with mixed peppers

ingredients

SERVES 4

1 tbsp vegetable or peanut oil

2 duck breasts, skin on

1 onion, sliced

2 garlic cloves, chopped

1 red pepper, deseeded and
    chopped

1 green pepper, deseeded
    and chopped

1 yellow pepper, deseeded
    and chopped

4 tomatoes, peeled, deseeded
    and chopped

150 ml/5 fl oz stock

3 tbsp Thai soy sauce

boiled noodles, garnished
    with chopped onion,
    to serve

method

1 Heat the oil in a wok and cook the duck
breasts over high heat until crisp and brown.
Turn over and cook until cooked through. Lift
out and keep warm.

2 Pour off any excess fat and stir-fry the onion
and garlic for 2–3 minutes, until softened and
lightly browned.

3 Add the peppers and stir-fry for 2–3
minutes, until tender. Add the tomatoes, stock
and soy sauce, and simmer for 1–2 minutes.
Transfer to a serving plate. Slice the duck
thickly and arrange on top, spooning any
sauce over it. Serve with noodles.

duck salad

ingredients

SERVES 4

4 boneless duck breasts,
    skin on
1 lemon grass stalk, broken
    into three and each cut in
    half lengthways
3 tbsp vegetable or peanut oil
2 tbsp sesame oil
1 tsp fish sauce
1 fresh green chilli, deseeded
    and chopped
2 tbsp Thai red curry paste
$1/2$ fresh pineapple, peeled
    and sliced
7.5-cm/3-inch piece
    cucumber, peeled,
    deseeded and sliced
3 tomatoes, cut into wedges
1 onion, sliced thinly

dressing
juice of 1 lemon
2 garlic cloves, crushed
1 tsp jaggery or soft light
    brown sugar
2 tbsp vegetable or peanut oil

method

1 Unwrap the duck and let the skin dry out overnight in the refrigerator.

2 The following day, slash the skin side 5 or 6 times. Mix the lemon grass, 2 tablespoons of the vegetable or peanut oil, all the sesame oil, fish sauce, chilli and curry paste together in a shallow dish and place the duck breasts in the mixture. Turn to coat and to rub the marinade into the meat. Chill for 2–3 hours.

3 Heat the remaining oil in a wok and cook the duck, skin-side down, over medium heat for 3–4 minutes until the skin is browned and crisp and the meat cooked most of the way through. Turn the breasts over and cook until browned and the meat is cooked to your liking.

4 Meanwhile, arrange the pineapple, cucumber, tomatoes and onions on a platter. Mix the dressing ingredients together and pour over the top.

5 Lift the duck out of the wok and slice thickly. Arrange the duck slices on top of the salad and serve while still hot.

fish & seafood

Fish and seafood are in plentiful supply in East Asia, so play an important role in the diet. They are given a similar treatment to meat and poultry, being cooked rapidly in a wok – steamed, deep-fried or stir-fried – with plenty of flavourings or a sauce added.

If you think of fish as being sometimes rather bland, you will soon change your mind when you try the recipes in this section – it takes on a new excitement when cooked, for example, with a lime and chilli sauce, or in a curry sauce. Or try Japanese-style fish cake, served with thick, round Udon noodles.

Choose fresh fish and cook it as soon as possible for the best flavour and quality. Recipes can be adapted to suit whatever fish is at its best, as long as it is from a similar 'family' to the variety specified. Fish can be quite delicate, so treat it gently, especially when you are adding a sauce – the flesh should keep its shape and texture, and not disintegrate, so it is often cooked separately, removed from the wok and returned to the remaining ingredients just to be warmed through. Scallops and squid should always be cooked until just tender – overcooking will make them tough. And king prawns need to retain their firm texture – expensive and therefore treated with great respect in China, they are very special served in a spicy ginger sauce.

monkfish with lime & chilli sauce

ingredients

SERVES 4

4 x 115-g/4-oz
   monkfish fillets
25 g/1 oz rice flour
   or cornflour
6 tbsp vegetable or peanut oil
4 garlic cloves, crushed
2 large fresh red chillies,
   deseeded and sliced
2 tsp jaggery or soft light
   brown sugar
juice of 2 limes
grated rind of 1 lime
boiled rice, to serve

method

1 Toss the fish in the flour, shaking off any excess. Heat the oil in a wok and cook the fish on all sides until browned and cooked through, taking care when turning not to break it up.

2 Lift the fish out of the wok and keep warm. Add the garlic and chillies and stir-fry for 1–2 minutes, until they have softened.

3 Add the sugar, the lime juice and rind and 2–3 tablespoons of water and bring to the boil. Simmer gently for 1–2 minutes, then spoon the mixture over the fish. Serve immediately with rice.

monkfish stir-fry

ingredients

SERVES 4

2 tsp sesame oil

450 g/1 lb monkfish steaks,
    cut into 2.5-cm/1-inch
    chunks

1 red onion, sliced thinly

3 cloves garlic, chopped
    finely

1 tsp grated fresh root ginger

225 g/8 oz fine tip asparagus

185 g/6 oz mushrooms,
    sliced thinly

2 tbsp soy sauce

1 tbsp lemon juice

lemon wedges, to garnish

cooked noodles, to serve

method

1 Heat the oil in a wok over medium-high heat. Add the fish, onion, garlic, root ginger, asparagus and mushrooms. Stir-fry for 2–3 minutes.

2 Stir in the soy sauce and lemon juice and cook for another minute. Remove from the heat and transfer to warm serving dishes.

3 Garnish with lemon wedges and serve immediately on a bed of cooked noodles.

fried fish with pine nuts

ingredients

SERVES 4–6

1/2 tsp salt

450 g/1 lb thick white fish
    fillets, cut into 2.5-cm/
    1-inch cubes

2 dried Chinese mushrooms,
    soaked in warm water
    for 20 minutes

3 tbsp vegetable or peanut oil

2.5-cm/1-inch piece of fresh
    root ginger, finely
    shredded

1 tbsp chopped spring onion

1 red pepper, cut into
    2.5-cm/1-inch squares

1 green pepper, cut into
    2.5-cm/1-inch squares

25 g/1 oz fresh or canned
    bamboo shoots, rinsed
    and cut into small cubes
    (if using fresh shoots, boil
    in water first for 30 minutes)

2 tsp Shaoxing rice wine

2 tbsp pine nuts, toasted

freshly cooked rice, to serve

method

1 Sprinkle the salt over the fish and set aside
for 20 minutes. Squeeze out any excess water
from the mushrooms and slice finely, discarding
any tough stems.

2 In a preheated wok, heat 2 tablespoons of
the oil and fry the fish for 3 minutes. Drain
and set aside.

3 In the clean, preheated wok, heat the
remaining oil and toss in the root ginger. Stir
until fragrant, then add the spring onion,
peppers, bamboo shoots, mushrooms and
Shaoxing and cook for 1–2 minutes.

4 Finally add the fish and stir to warm through.
Sprinkle with pine nuts and serve with freshly
cooked rice.

fish in coconut

ingredients

SERVES 4

2 tbsp vegetable or peanut oil

6 spring onions, chopped
    roughly

2.5-cm/1-inch piece fresh
    root ginger, grated

2–3 tbsp Thai red curry paste

400 ml/14 fl oz coconut milk

150 ml/5 fl oz fish stock

4 kaffir lime leaves

1 lemon grass stalk, broken
    in half

350 g/12 oz white fish fillets,
    skinned and cut into
    chunks

225 g/8 oz squid rings and
    tentacles

225 g/8 oz large cooked
    peeled prawns

1 tbsp fish sauce

2 tbsp Thai soy sauce

4 tbsp chopped fresh Chinese
    chives

boiled jasmine rice with
    chopped fresh coriander,
    to serve

method

1 Heat the oil in a wok and stir-fry the spring onions and root ginger for 1–2 minutes. Add the curry paste and stir-fry for 1–2 minutes.

2 Add the coconut milk, fish stock, lime leaves and lemon grass. Bring to the boil, then reduce the heat and simmer for 1 minute.

3 Add the fish, squid and prawns, and simmer for 2–3 minutes, until the fish is cooked. Add the fish and soy sauces and stir in the chives. Serve immediately with jasmine rice with fresh coriander stirred through it.

chillies stuffed with fish paste

ingredients

SERVES 4–6

225 g/8 oz white fish, minced

2 tbsp lightly beaten egg

4–6 mild red and green chillies

vegetable or peanut oil, for shallow-frying

2 garlic cloves, finely chopped

1/2 tsp fermented black beans, rinsed and lightly mashed

1 tbsp light soy sauce

pinch of sugar

1 tbsp water

marinade

1 tsp finely chopped fresh root ginger

pinch of salt

pinch of white pepper

1/2 tsp vegetable or peanut oil

method

1 Combine all the marinade ingredients in a bowl and marinate the fish for 20 minutes. Add the egg and mix by hand to create a smooth paste.

2 To prepare the chillies, cut in half lengthways and scoop out the seeds and loose flesh. Cut into bite-size pieces. Spread each piece of chilli with about 1/2 teaspoon of the fish paste.

3 In a preheated wok, heat plenty of the oil and cook the chilli pieces on both sides until beginning to turn golden brown. Drain and set aside.

4 Heat 1 tablespoon of the oil in the clean wok and stir-fry the garlic until aromatic. Stir in the black beans and mix well. Add the light soy sauce and sugar and stir, then add the chilli pieces. Add the water, then cover and simmer over low heat for 5 minutes. Serve immediately.

five-willow fish

ingredients

SERVES 4–6

1 whole sea bass or similar,
    weighing 450–675 g/
    1–1^1/$_2$ lb, gutted

2 tsp salt

6 tbsp vegetable or peanut oil

2 slices fresh root ginger

2 garlic cloves, finely sliced

2 spring onions, roughly
    chopped

1 green pepper, thinly sliced

1 red pepper, thinly sliced

1 carrot, finely sliced

55 g/2 oz fresh or canned
    bamboo shoots, rinsed
    and thinly sliced (if using
    fresh shoots, boil in water
    first for 30 minutes)

2 tomatoes, peeled, deseeded
    and thinly sliced

1 tbsp Shaoxing rice wine

2 tbsp white rice vinegar

1 tbsp light soy sauce

1 tbsp sugar

method

1 Clean the fish and dry thoroughly. Score the fish on both sides with deep, diagonal cuts. Press ^{1}/$_2$ teaspoon of the salt into the skin.

2 In a preheated wok, heat 4 tablespoons of the oil and cook the fish for about 4 minutes on each side, or until the flesh is soft. Drain, then set aside and keep warm.

3 In the clean preheated wok, heat the remaining oil and stir-fry the root ginger, garlic and spring onions until fragrant. Toss in the vegetables with the remaining salt and stir rapidly for 2–3 minutes. Add the remaining ingredients and mix well for 2–3 minutes. Pour the sauce over the fish and serve at once.

fish curry

ingredients

SERVES 4

juice of 1 lime

4 tbsp fish sauce

2 tbsp Thai soy sauce

1 fresh red chilli, deseeded
    and chopped

350 g/12 oz monkfish fillet,
    cut into cubes

350 g/12 oz salmon fillets,
    skinned and cut into
    cubes

400 ml/14 fl oz coconut milk

3 kaffir lime leaves

1 tbsp Thai red curry paste

1 lemon grass stalk (white
    part only), chopped finely

2 cups jasmine rice, boiled

4 tbsp chopped fresh
    coriander

method

1 Combine the lime juice, half the fish sauce
and the soy sauce in a shallow, non-metallic
dish. Add the chilli and the fish, stir to coat,
cover with clingfilm and chill for 1–2 hours,
or overnight.

2 Bring the coconut milk to the boil in a wok and
add the lime leaves, curry paste, the remaining
fish sauce and the lemon grass. Simmer gently
for 10–15 minutes.

3 Add the fish and the marinade and simmer
for 4–5 minutes, until the fish is cooked. Serve
hot with boiled rice with chopped coriander
stirred through it.

mixed seafood curry

ingredients

SERVES 4

1 tbsp vegetable or peanut oil

3 shallots, chopped finely

2.5-cm/1-inch piece fresh
    galangal, peeled and
    sliced thinly

2 garlic cloves, chopped finely

400 ml/14 fl oz canned
    coconut milk

2 lemon grass stalks,
    snapped in half

4 tbsp fish sauce

2 tbsp chilli sauce

225 g/8 oz uncooked king
    prawns, peeled

225 g/8 oz baby squid,
    cleaned and sliced thickly

225 g/8 oz salmon fillet,
    skinned and cut into
    chunks

175 g/6 oz tuna steak, cut
    into chunks

225 g/8 oz fresh mussels,
    scrubbed and debearded

fresh Chinese chives,
    to garnish

boiled rice, to serve

method

1 Heat the oil in a large wok and stir-fry the shallots, galangal and garlic for 1–2 minutes, until they start to soften. Add the coconut milk, lemon grass, fish sauce and chilli sauce. Bring to the boil, reduce the heat, and simmer for 1–2 minutes.

2 Add the prepared prawns, squid, salmon and tuna, and simmer for 3–4 minutes, until the prawns have turned pink and the fish is cooked.

3 Add the mussels to the wok and cover with a lid. Simmer for 1–2 minutes, until they have opened. Discard any mussels that remain closed. Garnish with Chinese chives and serve immediately with rice.

spicy thai seafood stew

ingredients

SERVES 4

200 g/7 oz squid, cleaned
and tentacles discarded

500 g/1 lb 2 oz firm white fish
fillet, preferably monkfish
or halibut

1 tbsp corn oil

4 shallots, finely chopped

2 garlic cloves, finely chopped

2 tbsp Thai green curry paste

2 small lemon grass stems,
finely chopped

1 tsp shrimp paste

500 ml/16 fl oz coconut milk

200 g/7 oz raw king prawns,
peeled and deveined

12 live clams in shells, cleaned

8 fresh basil leaves, finely
shredded

fresh basil leaves, to garnish

freshly cooked rice, to serve

method

1 Using a sharp knife, cut the squid body cavities into thick rings and the white fish into bite-size chunks.

2 Heat the oil in a large preheated wok. Add the shallots, garlic and curry paste and stir-fry for 1–2 minutes. Add the lemon grass and shrimp paste, then stir in the coconut milk and bring to the boil.

3 Reduce the heat until the liquid is simmering gently, then add the white fish, squid and prawns to the wok and simmer for 2 minutes.

4 Add the clams and simmer for a further 1 minute, or until the clams have opened. Discard any clams that remain closed.

5 Sprinkle the shredded basil leaves over the stew. Transfer to serving plates, then garnish with whole basil leaves and serve immediately with rice.

spicy scallops with lime & chilli

ingredients

SERVES 4

16 large scallops, shelled
1 tbsp butter
1 tbsp vegetable oil
1 tsp crushed garlic
1 tsp grated fresh root ginger
1 bunch of spring onions,
    finely sliced
finely grated rind of 1 lime
1 small fresh red chilli,
    deseeded and very finely
    chopped
3 tbsp lime juice
lime wedges, to garnish
freshly cooked rice, to serve

method

1 Using a sharp knife, trim the scallops to remove any black intestine, then wash and pat dry with kitchen paper. Separate the corals from the white parts, then slice each white part in half horizontally, making 2 circles.

2 Heat the butter and oil in a preheated wok. Add the garlic and root ginger and stir-fry for 1 minute without browning. Add the spring onions and stir-fry for 1 minute.

3 Add the scallops and continue stir-frying over high heat for 4–5 minutes. Stir in the lime rind, chilli and lime juice and cook for a further 1 minute.

4 Transfer the scallops to serving plates, then spoon over the cooking juices and garnish with lime wedges. Serve hot with freshly cooked rice.

stir-fried scallops with asparagus

ingredients

SERVES 4

225 g/8 oz scallops

2 tsp salt

225 g/8 oz asparagus

3 tbsp vegetable or peanut oil

55 g/2 oz fresh or canned
   bamboo shoots, rinsed
   and thinly sliced (if using
   fresh shoots, boil in water
   first for 30 minutes)

1 small carrot, finely sliced

4 thin slices of fresh root
   ginger

pinch of white pepper

2 tbsp Shaoxing rice wine

2 tbsp chicken stock

1 tsp sesame oil

method

1 Sprinkle the scallops with 1 teaspoon of the salt and set aside for 20 minutes.

2 Trim the asparagus, discarding the tough ends. Cut into 5-cm/2-inch pieces and blanch in a large pan of boiling water for 30 seconds. Drain and set aside.

3 In a preheated wok, heat 1 tablespoon of the oil and cook the scallops for 30 seconds. Drain and set aside.

4 In the clean wok, heat another tablespoon of the oil and stir-fry the asparagus, bamboo shoots and carrot for 2 minutes. Season with the remaining salt. Drain and set aside.

5 In the clean wok, heat the remaining oil, then add the root ginger and stir-fry until fragrant. Return the scallops and vegetables to the wok and sprinkle with the pepper, Shaoxing and stock. Cover and continue cooking for 2 minutes, then toss through the sesame oil and serve.

scallops in black bean sauce

ingredients

SERVES 4

2 tbsp vegetable or peanut oil

1 tsp finely chopped garlic

1 tsp finely chopped fresh
   root ginger

1 tbsp fermented black beans,
   rinsed and lightly mashed

400 g/14 oz scallops

$^1/_2$ tsp light soy sauce

1 tsp Shaoxing rice wine

1 tsp sugar

3–4 red Thai chillies, finely
   chopped

1–2 tsp chicken stock

1 tbsp finely chopped
   spring onion

method

1 In a preheated wok, heat the oil. Add the garlic and stir, then add the root ginger and stir-fry together for about 1 minute, or until fragrant. Mix in the black beans, then toss in the scallops and stir-fry for 1 minute. Add the light soy sauce, Shaoxing, sugar and chillies.

2 Lower the heat and simmer for 2 minutes, adding the stock if necessary. Finally add the spring onion, then stir and serve.

squid & red peppers

ingredients

SERVES 4

spice paste

2 tbsp vegetable or peanut oil

1 tbsp chilli oil with shrimp

2 shallots, chopped

2–3 large fresh red chillies,
    deseeded and chopped
    roughly

2 tbsp ground coriander

2 tbsp ground cumin

1-inch piece fresh root ginger,
    chopped

1 tbsp finely chopped lemon
    grass

3–4 coriander roots, chopped

1 tsp salt

1 tsp jaggery or soft light
    brown sugar

stir-fry

2 red peppers, deseeded
    and diced

150 ml/5 fl oz plain yogurt

750 g/1 lb 10 oz squid,
    cleaned and sliced

juice of 1 lime

115 g/4 oz block creamed
    coconut, chopped

150 ml/5 fl oz hot water

freshly cooked rice, to serve

method

1 Put all the ingredients for the spice paste into a food processor and process until chopped finely.

2 Scrape the spice paste into a wok and stir-fry gently for 3–4 minutes. Add the red peppers and stir-fry for 1–2 minutes.

3 Add the yogurt and bring to the boil. Add the squid and simmer for 2–3 minutes, then stir in the lime juice, coconut and water. Simmer for a further 1–2 minutes, until the coconut dissolves. Serve immediately.with freshly cooked rice.

stir-fried squid with hot black bean sauce

ingredients

SERVES 4

750 g/1 lb 10 oz squid,
    cleaned and tentacles
    discarded
1 large red pepper, deseeded
115 g/4 oz mangetout
1 head of pak choi
3 tbsp black bean sauce
1 tbsp Thai fish sauce
1 tbsp rice wine or dry sherry
1 tbsp dark soy sauce
1 tsp brown sugar
1 tsp cornflour
1 tbsp water
1 tbsp corn oil
1 tsp sesame oil
1 small fresh red Thai chilli,
    chopped
1 garlic clove, finely chopped
1 tsp grated fresh root ginger
2 spring onions, chopped

method

1 Cut the squid body cavities into quarters lengthways. Use the tip of a small, sharp knife to score a diamond pattern into the flesh, without cutting all the way through. Pat dry with kitchen paper.

2 Cut the pepper into long, thin slices. Cut the mangetout in half diagonally. Coarsely shred the pak choi.

3 Mix the black bean sauce, fish sauce, rice wine, soy sauce and sugar together in a bowl. Blend the cornflour with the water and stir into the other sauce ingredients. Reserve the mixture until required.

4 Heat the oils in a preheated wok. Add the chilli, garlic, root ginger and spring onions and stir-fry for 1 minute. Add the pepper slices and stir-fry for 2 minutes.

5 Add the squid and stir-fry over high heat for a further 1 minute. Stir in the mangetout and pak choi and stir for a further 1 minute, or until wilted.

6 Stir in the sauce ingredients and cook, stirring constantly, for 2 minutes, or until the sauce thickens and clears. Serve immediately.

prawns with spring onions & straw mushrooms

ingredients

SERVES 4

2 tbsp vegetable or peanut oil

bunch of spring onions, chopped

2 garlic cloves, chopped finely

175 g/6 oz block creamed coconut, chopped roughly

2 tbsp Thai red curry paste

450 ml/15 fl oz fish stock

2 tbsp fish sauce

2 tbsp Thai soy sauce

6 sprigs fresh Thai basil

400 g/14 oz canned straw mushrooms, drained

350 g/12 oz large cooked peeled prawns

boiled jasmine rice, to serve

method

1 Heat the oil in a wok and stir-fry the spring onions and garlic for 2–3 minutes. Add the creamed coconut, red curry paste and stock, and heat gently, stirring, until the coconut has dissolved.

2 Stir in the fish sauce and soy sauce, then add the basil, mushrooms and prawns. Gradually bring to the boil and serve at once with jasmine rice.

prawns fu yung

ingredients

SERVES 4–6

1 tbsp vegetable or peanut oil

115 g/4 oz raw prawns,
    peeled and deveined

4 eggs, lightly beaten

1 tsp salt

pinch of white pepper

2 tbsp finely chopped
    Chinese chives

method

1 In a preheated wok, heat the oil and stir-fry the prawns until they begin to turn pink.

2 Season the beaten eggs with the salt and pepper and pour over the prawns. Stir-fry for 1 minute, then add the chives.

3 Cook for a further 4 minutes, stirring all the time, until the eggs are cooked through but still soft in texture, and serve immediately.

wok-fried jumbo prawns in spicy sauce

ingredients

SERVES 4

3 tbsp vegetable or peanut oil

450 g/1 lb raw king prawns, deveined but unpeeled

2 tsp finely chopped fresh root ginger

1 tsp finely chopped garlic

1 tbsp chopped spring onion

2 tbsp chilli bean sauce

1 tsp Shaoxing rice wine

1 tsp sugar

$^1/_2$ tsp light soy sauce

1–2 tbsp chicken stock

method

1 In a preheated wok, heat the oil, then toss in the prawns and stir-fry over high heat for about 4 minutes. Arrange the prawns on the sides of the wok out of the oil, then throw in the root ginger and garlic and stir until fragrant. Add the spring onion and chilli bean sauce. Stir the prawns into this mixture.

2 Lower the heat slightly and add the Shaoxing, sugar, light soy sauce and a little chicken stock. Cover and cook for a further minute. Serve immediately.

somen noodles with prawns

ingredients

SERVES 2

1 tbsp oil

16 raw prawns, peeled
   and deveined

3 shiitake mushrooms,
   finely sliced

1/4 white or green cabbage,
   shredded

1 carrot, shredded

2 bundles of somen noodles

6 shiso leaves, shredded

dressing

3 tbsp oil

1 tbsp sesame seeds, toasted

125 ml/4 fl oz Japanese
   rice vinegar

1 tbsp sugar

1 tbsp usukuchi shoyu
   (Japanese light soy sauce)

salt

method

1 To make the dressing, mix all the dressing ingredients together, with salt to taste, in a non-metallic bowl.

2 Preheat a wok over high heat. Add the remaining oil and heat until very hot. Add the prawns and cook, tossing occasionally, until they have turned pink.

3 Add the mushrooms to the wok and stir-fry for 1 minute, then add the cabbage and carrot and toss together. Remove from the heat and set aside to cool.

4 Cook the noodles according to the packet instructions, then drain. Put in a large bowl with the prawn mixture. Add the dressing and toss well. Sprinkle with the shiso leaves and serve.

stir-fried fresh crab with ginger

ingredients

SERVES 4

3 tbsp vegetable or peanut oil

2 large fresh crabs, cleaned,
    broken into pieces and legs
    cracked with a cleaver

55 g/2 oz fresh root ginger,
    julienned

100 g/3^1/$_2$ oz spring onions,
    chopped into 5-cm/2-inch
    lengths

2 tbsp light soy sauce

1 tsp sugar

pinch of white pepper

method

1 In a preheated wok, heat 2 tablespoons of the oil and cook the crab over high heat for 3–4 minutes. Remove and set aside.

2 In the clean wok, heat the remaining oil, then toss in the root ginger and stir until fragrant. Add the spring onions, then stir in the crab pieces. Add the light soy sauce, sugar and pepper. Cover and simmer for 1 minute and serve immediately.

clams in black bean sauce

ingredients

SERVES 4

900 g/2 lb small clams

1 tbsp vegetable or peanut oil

1 tsp finely chopped fresh
    root ginger

1 tsp finely chopped garlic

1 tbsp fermented black beans,
    rinsed and roughly
    chopped

2 tsp Shaoxing rice wine

1 tbsp finely chopped spring
    onion

1 tsp salt (optional)

method

1 Start by washing the clams thoroughly, then soak them in clean water until it is time to drain them and toss them in the wok.

2 In a preheated wok, heat the oil and stir-fry the root ginger and garlic until fragrant. Add the black beans and cook for 1 minute.

3 Over high heat, add the clams and Shaoxing and stir-fry for 2 minutes to mix everything together. Cover and cook for about 3 minutes. Add the spring onion and salt, if necessary, and serve immediately.

udon noodle stir-fry with fish cake & ginger

ingredients

SERVES 2

2 x 150-g/5^{1}/$_2$-oz packs
　ready-to-wok udon
　noodles

1 leek, shredded

175 g/6 oz bean sprouts

8 shiitake mushrooms,
　finely sliced

2 pieces Japanese fish
　cake, sliced

12 raw prawns, peeled
　and deveined

2 eggs, beaten

oil, for stir-frying

2 tbsp shoyu (Japanese
　soy sauce)

3 tbsp mirin

2 tbsp chopped fresh
　coriander leaves

chilli oil

sesame oil

2 spring onions, finely sliced

2 tbsp shredded beni-shoga
　(red ginger), to serve

method

1 Rinse the noodles under cold running water to remove any oil and tip into a bowl.

2 Add the leek, bean sprouts, mushrooms, fish cake, prawns and eggs to the noodles and mix well to combine.

3 Preheat a wok over high heat. Add a little oil and heat until very hot. Add the noodle mixture and stir-fry until golden, and the prawns have turned pink and are cooked through.

4 Add the soy sauce, mirin and coriander and toss together. Divide the noodles between 2 bowls, drizzle with the chilli and sesame oils, and sprinkle over the spring onions and beni-shoga. Serve immediately.

rice &
noodles

Rice and noodles are the two staples of Eastern Asian cuisine and form an excellent base for stir-fried dishes. Rice is grown in this region, and Thai people in particular consume huge quantities – it is estimated that, on average, each of them eats about 500 g/ 1 lb 2 oz every day.

Noodles are eaten by the Thais, Chinese and Japanese alike and there is a remarkable range available. Some are made, like Italian pasta, from wheat, but they are also made from rice flour, buckwheat (which, unlike wheat, is not a grain but a nut) or ground mung beans. Each variety takes on a different appearance once cooked – 'cellophane' or bean thread noodles, for example, made from mung beans, become glossy, while rice noodles, translucent when raw, turn a matt white.

Rice and noodles are naturally low in fat, so these recipes are perfect for those who are keeping an eye on their health. And if you have children who are fussy eaters, the solution must surely be to serve them a simple but hearty Chinese family dish with the most appealing name – 'Ants Climbing a Tree'. It is said to have been so called because the pieces of minced meat cling to the noodles, resembling an army of ants on the march!

egg fu yung

ingredients

SERVES 4–6

2 eggs

1/2 tsp salt

pinch of white pepper

1 tsp melted butter

2 tbsp vegetable or peanut oil

1 tsp finely chopped garlic

1 small onion, finely sliced

1 green pepper, finely sliced

450 g/1 lb cooked rice, chilled

1 tbsp light soy sauce

1 tbsp finely chopped spring onion

140 g/5 oz bean sprouts, trimmed

2 drops of sesame oil

method

1 Beat the eggs with the salt and pepper. Heat the butter in a pan and pour in the eggs. Cook as an omelette, until set, then remove from the pan and cut into slivers.

2 In a preheated wok, heat the oil and stir-fry the garlic until fragrant. Add the onion and stir-fry for 1 minute, then add the green pepper and stir for 1 more minute. Stir in the rice and when the grains are separated, stir in the light soy sauce and cook for 1 minute.

3 Add the spring onion and egg strips and stir well, then finally add the bean sprouts and sesame oil. Stir-fry for 1 minute and serve.

egg-fried rice

ingredients

SERVES 4

2 tbsp vegetable or peanut oil

350 g/12 oz cooked rice,
    chilled

1 egg, well beaten

method

1 Heat the oil in a preheated wok and stir-fry the rice for 1 minute, breaking it down as much as possible into individual grains.

2 Quickly add the egg, stirring, so as to coat each piece of rice. Stir until the egg is cooked and the rice, as far as possible, is in single grains. Serve immediately.

egg-fried rice with chicken

ingredients

SERVES 4

225 g/8 oz jasmine rice

3 skinless, boneless chicken
breasts, cut into cubes

400 ml/14 fl oz canned
coconut milk

50 g/1¾ oz block creamed
coconut, chopped

2–3 coriander roots, chopped

thinly pared rind of 1 lemon

1 fresh green chilli, deseeded
and chopped

3 fresh Thai basil leaves

1 tbsp fish sauce

1 tbsp oil

3 eggs, beaten

fresh chives and
sprigs of fresh coriander,
for the garnish

method

1 Cook the rice in boiling water for 12–15
minutes, drain well and cool, then chill in the
refrigerator overnight.

2 Put the chicken in a saucepan and cover
with the coconut milk. Add the creamed
coconut, coriander roots, lemon rind and chilli
and bring to the boil. Simmer for 8–10 minutes,
until the chicken is tender. Remove from the
heat. Stir in the basil and fish sauce.

3 Meanwhile, heat the oil in a wok and stir-fry
the rice for 2–3 minutes. Pour in the eggs and
stir until they have cooked and mixed with the
rice. Line 4 small ovenproof bowls or ramekins
with clingfilm and pack with the rice. Turn out
carefully onto serving plates and remove the
clingfilm. Garnish with long chives and sprigs
of coriander. Serve with the chicken.

egg-fried rice with vegetables & crispy onions

ingredients

SERVES 4

4 tbsp vegetable or peanut oil

2 garlic cloves, chopped finely

2 fresh red chillies, deseeded
and chopped

115 g/4 oz mushrooms, sliced

55 g/2 oz mangetout, halved

55 g/2 oz baby corn cobs,
halved

3 tbsp Thai soy sauce

1 tbsp jaggery or soft light
brown sugar

few Thai basil leaves

350 g/12 oz rice, cooked and
cooled

2 eggs, beaten

2 onions, sliced

method

1 Heat half the oil in a wok and sauté the garlic and chillies for 2–3 minutes.

2 Add the mushrooms, mangetout and corn and stir-fry for 2–3 minutes before adding the soy sauce, sugar and basil. Stir in the rice.

3 Push the mixture to one side of the wok and add the eggs to the bottom. Stir until lightly set before combining into the rice mixture.

4 Heat the remaining oil in another wok and sauté the onions until crispy and brown. Serve the rice topped with the onions.

dan dan mian

ingredients

SERVES 4

1 tbsp vegetable or peanut oil

1 large dried chilli, deseeded
    and snipped into 3 pieces

1/2 tsp Sichuan peppers

100 g/3 1/2 oz minced beef

2 tsp light soy sauce

300 g/10 1/2 oz fine white
    noodles

1 tbsp roasted peanuts,
    chopped

sauce

1 tbsp preserved vegetables

1/2 tsp Sichuan peppers,
    lightly roasted and crushed

100 ml/3 1/2 fl oz chicken
    stock

1 tsp black Chinese vinegar

1 tsp chilli oil

1 tsp dark soy sauce

1 tbsp light soy sauce

1 tbsp sesame paste

few drops of sesame oil

2 spring onions, finely
    chopped

method

1 Heat the oil in a preheated wok and toss in the chilli and peppers, then add the meat and stir rapidly. When the meat has changed colour, add the light soy sauce and continue to cook until the meat is well browned. Carefully mix the sauce ingredients together and pour into 4 noodle bowls.

2 Cook the noodles according to the directions on the packet. When cooked, drain and divide among the bowls.

3 Top with the meat mixture, then sprinkle with the roasted peanuts and serve at once. Mix well before eating.

beef chow mein

ingredients

SERVES 4

280 g/10 oz tenderloin steak,
  cut into slivers

225 g/8 oz dried egg noodles

2 tbsp vegetable or peanut oil

1 onion, finely sliced

1 green pepper, finely sliced

140 g/5 oz bean sprouts,
  trimmed

1 tsp salt

pinch of sugar

2 tsp Shaoxing rice wine

2 tbsp light soy sauce

1 tbsp dark soy sauce

1 tbsp finely shredded spring
  onion

marinade

1 tsp light soy sauce

dash of sesame oil

$1/2$ tsp Shaoxing rice wine

pinch of white pepper

method

1 Combine all the marinade ingredients in a bowl and marinate the beef for at least 20 minutes.

2 Cook the noodles according to the directions on the packet. When cooked, rinse under cold water and set aside.

3 In a preheated wok, heat the oil and stir-fry the beef for about 1 minute, or until the meat has changed colour, then add the onion and cook for 1 minute, followed by the pepper and bean sprouts. Evaporate off any water from the vegetables. Add the salt, sugar, Shaoxing and soy sauces. Stir in the noodles and toss for 1 minute. Finally, stir in the spring onion and serve.

fried rice
with pork & prawns

ingredients

SERVES 4

3 tsp vegetable or peanut oil

1 egg, lightly beaten

100 g/3^1/$_2$ oz raw prawns, peeled, deveined and cut into 2 pieces

100 g/3^1/$_2$ oz cha siu, finely chopped

2 tbsp finely chopped spring onion

200 g/7 oz cooked rice, chilled

1 tsp salt

method

1 In a preheated wok, heat 1 teaspoon of the oil and pour in the egg. Cook until scrambled. Remove and set aside.

2 Add the remaining oil and stir-fry the prawns, cha siu and spring onion for about 2 minutes. Add the rice and salt, breaking up the rice into grains, and cook for a further 2 minutes. Finally, stir in the cooked egg. Serve at once.

pork lo mein

ingredients

SERVES 4–6

175 g/6 oz boneless lean
    pork, shredded

225 g/8 oz egg noodles

1½ tbsp vegetable or
    peanut oil

2 tsp finely chopped garlic

1 tsp finely chopped fresh
    root ginger

1 carrot, julienned

225 g/8 oz finely
    sliced mushrooms

1 green pepper, thinly sliced

1 tsp salt

175 ml/6 fl oz hot chicken
    stock

200 g/7 oz bean sprouts,
    trimmed

2 tbsp finely chopped spring
    onion

marinade

1 tsp light soy sauce

dash of sesame oil

pinch of white pepper

method

1 Combine all the marinade ingredients in
a bowl and marinate the pork for at least
20 minutes.

2 Cook the noodles according to the directions
on the packet. When cooked, drain and then
set aside.

3 In a preheated wok, heat 1 teaspoon of the
oil and stir-fry the pork until the colour has
changed. Remove and set aside.

4 In the clean wok, heat the remaining oil and
stir-fry the garlic and root ginger until fragrant.
Add the carrot and cook for 1 minute, then
add the mushrooms and cook for 1 minute.
Toss in the pepper and cook for 1 minute. Add
the pork, salt and stock and heat through.
Finally, toss in the noodles, followed by the
bean sprouts, and stir well. Sprinkle with the
spring onion and serve.

prawns with coconut rice

ingredients

SERVES 4

115 g/4 oz dried Chinese
    mushrooms

2 tbsp vegetable or peanut oil

6 spring onions, chopped

55 g/2 oz dessicated coconut

1 fresh green chilli, deseeded
    and chopped

225 g/8 oz jasmine rice

150 ml/5 fl oz fish stock

400 ml/14 fl oz coconut milk

350 g/12 oz cooked
    peeled prawns

6 sprigs fresh Thai basil

method

1 Place the mushrooms in a small bowl, cover with hot water and set aside to soak for 30 minutes. Drain, then cut off and discard the stalks and slice the caps.

2 Heat 1 tablespoon of the oil in a wok and stir-fry the spring onions, coconut and chilli for 2–3 minutes, until lightly browned. Add the mushrooms and stir-fry for 3–4 minutes.

3 Add the rice and stir-fry for 2–3 minutes, then add the stock and bring to the boil. Reduce the heat and add the coconut milk. simmer for 10–15 minutes, until the rice is tender. Stir in the prawns and basil, heat through and serve.

rice with seafood & squid

ingredients

SERVES 4

2 tbsp vegetable or peanut oil

3 shallots, chopped finely

2 garlic cloves, chopped
    finely

225 g/8 oz jasmine rice

300 ml/10 fl oz fish stock

4 spring onions, chopped

2 tbsp Thai red curry paste

225 g/8 oz baby squid,
    cleaned and sliced thickly

225 g/8 oz white fish fillets,
    skinned and cut into
    cubes

225 g/8 oz salmon fillets,
    skinned and cut into
    cubes

4 tbsp chopped fresh
    coriander

method

1 Heat 1 tablespoon of the oil in a wok and stir-fry the shallots and garlic for 2–3 minutes, until softened. Add the rice and stir-fry for 2–3 minutes.

2 Add a ladleful of the stock and simmer, adding more stock as needed, for 12–15 minutes, until tender. Transfer to a dish and cool, then chill in the refrigerator overnight.

3 Heat the remaining oil in a wok and stir-fry the spring onions and curry paste for 2–3 minutes. Add the squid and fish and stir-fry gently to avoid breaking up the fish. Stir in the rice and coriander, heat through gently and serve.

beef with fresh noodles

ingredients

SERVES 4

6 dried black cloud Chinese
    mushrooms

2 tbsp vegetable or peanut oil

2 x 225-g/8-oz sirloin steaks,
    sliced thickly

1 onion, cut into thin wedges

2 garlic cloves, chopped

1 green pepper, deseeded
    and chopped

3 celery stalks, sliced

2 tbsp Thai green curry paste

300 ml/10 fl oz beef stock

4 tbsp black bean sauce

225 g/8 oz fresh egg noodles

4 tbsp chopped fresh parsley

method

1 Put the dried mushrooms in a bowl, cover with boiling water and soak for 30 minutes. Drain, then break up any larger pieces.

2 Heat the oil in a wok and stir-fry the steak over high heat until browned. Add the mushrooms, onion, garlic, pepper and celery and stir-fry for 3–4 minutes. Add the curry paste, beef stock and black bean sauce and stir-fry for 2–3 minutes.

3 Meanwhile, cook the noodles in boiling water for 3–4 minutes, drain well and stir into the wok. Sprinkle the parsley over and stir. Serve immediately.

rice noodles with beef in black bean sauce

ingredients

SERVES 4–6

225 g/8 oz rump steak,
    finely sliced
225 g/8 oz rice sticks
2–3 tbsp vegetable or
    peanut oil
1 small onion, finely sliced
1 green pepper, finely sliced
1 red pepper, finely sliced
2 tbsp black bean sauce
2–3 tbsp light soy sauce

marinade

1 tbsp dark soy sauce
1 tsp Shaoxing rice wine
$^1/_2$ tsp sugar
$^1/_2$ tsp white pepper

method

1 Combine all the marinade ingredients in a bowl and marinate the beef for at least 20 minutes.

2 Cook the rice sticks according to the directions on the packet. When cooked, drain and set aside.

3 In a preheated wok, heat the oil and stir-fry the beef for 1 minute, or until the meat has changed colour. Drain the meat and set aside.

4 Pour off any excess oil from the wok and stir-fry the onion and peppers for 1 minute. Add the black bean sauce and stir well, then pour in the light soy sauce. Toss the rice sticks in the vegetables and, when fully incorporated, add the beef and stir until warmed through. Serve immediately.

ants climbing a tree

ingredients

SERVES 4–6

55 g/2 oz minced beef

55 g/2 oz minced pork

1 tbsp light soy sauce

pinch of salt

1 tbsp vegetable or peanut oil

1 tbsp chilli bean paste

1 tsp dark soy sauce

175 ml/6 fl oz hot chicken
stock

140 g/5 oz beanthread
noodles, soaked in warm
water for 20 minutes
and drained

2 spring onions, finely
chopped

method

1 Combine the minced meats with 1 teaspoon of the light soy sauce and the salt.

2 In a preheated wok, heat the oil and cook the minced meats until beginning to brown. Add the chilli paste and stir rapidly. Stir in the dark soy sauce.

3 Pour in the stock, noodles and remaining light soy sauce. Cover the wok and simmer for about 8–10 minutes, or until the wok is quite dry. Shake the wok but do not stir. Toss in the spring onions and serve.

sour & spicy pork

ingredients

SERVES 4

55 g/2 oz dried Chinese cloud
ear mushrooms

100 g/3$^{1}/_{2}$ oz baby corn,
halved lengthways

2 tbsp honey

1 tbsp tamarind paste

4 tbsp boiling water

2 tbsp dark soy sauce

1 tbsp rice vinegar

2 tbsp peanut or corn oil

1 large garlic clove, very finely
chopped

1-cm/$^{1}/_{2}$-inch piece fresh root
ginger, peeled and very
finely chopped

$^{1}/_{2}$ tsp dried red pepper
flakes, or to taste

350 g/12 oz pork fillet,
thinly sliced

4 spring onions, thickly sliced
on the diagonal

1 green pepper, cored,
deseeded and sliced

250 g/9 oz fresh Hokkien
noodles

chopped fresh coriander,
to garnish

method

1 Soak the mushrooms in enough boiling water to cover for 20 minutes, or until they are tender. Drain them well, then cut off and discard any thick stems, and slice the cups if they are large. Meanwhile, bring a large saucepan of lightly salted water to the boil, add the baby corn and blanch for 3 minutes. Drain the corn and run it under cold running water to stop the cooking, then set aside. Put the honey and tamarind paste in a small bowl and stir in the water, stirring until the paste dissolves. Stir in the soy sauce and rice vinegar and set aside.

2 Heat a wok over high heat. Add 1 tablespoon of the oil and heat until it shimmers. Add the garlic, root ginger and red pepper flakes and stir-fry for about 30 seconds. Add the pork and continue stir-frying for 2 minutes.

3 Add the remaining oil to the wok and heat. Add the spring onions, pepper, mushrooms and baby corn, along with the tamarind mixture, and stir-fry for a further 2–3 minutes, until the pork is cooked through and the vegetables are tender, but still firm to the bite. Add the noodles and use 2 forks to mix all the ingredients together. When the noodles and sauce are hot, sprinkle with coriander.

pad thai

ingredients

SERVES 4

225 g/8 oz thick rice-stick
    noodles
2 tbsp vegetable or peanut oil
2 garlic cloves, chopped
2 fresh red chillies, deseeded
    and chopped
175 g/6 oz pork fillet,
    sliced thinly
115 g/4 oz uncooked prawns,
    peeled and chopped
8 fresh Chinese chives,
    chopped
2 tbsp fish sauce
juice of 1 lime
2 tsp jaggery or soft light
    brown sugar
2 eggs, beaten
115 g/4 oz bean sprouts
4 tbsp chopped fresh
    coriander
115 g/4 oz unsalted peanuts,
    chopped, plus extra to serve
crispy fried onions, to serve

method

1 Soak the noodles in warm water for
10 minutes, drain well and set aside.

2 Heat the oil in a wok and stir-fry the garlic,
chillies and pork for 2–3 minutes. Add the
prawns to the wok and stir-fry for a further
2–3 minutes.

3 Add the chives and noodles, then cover
and cook for 1–2 minutes. Add the fish sauce,
lime juice, sugar and eggs. Cook, stirring and
tossing constantly to mix in the eggs.

4 Stir in the bean sprouts, coriander and
peanuts, and serve with small dishes of crispy
fried onions and extra chopped peanuts.

noodle baskets
with chicken lime salad

ingredients

SERVES 4

peanut or corn oil, for
    deep-frying
250 g/9 oz fresh thin or
    medium Chinese egg
    noodles

chicken-lime salad

6 tbsp sour cream
6 tbsp mayonnaise
2.5-cm/1-inch piece fresh
    root ginger, peeled and
    grated
grated rind and juice of 1 lime
4 skinless, boneless chicken
    thighs, poached and cooled,
    then cut into thin strips
1 carrot, peeled and grated
1 cucumber, cut in half
    lengthways, seeds
    removed and sliced
salt and pepper
1 tbsp finely chopped fresh
    coriander
1 tbsp finely chopped
    fresh mint
1 tbsp finely chopped fresh
    parsley
several fresh basil leaves, torn

method

1 To shape noodle baskets, you will need a
special set of 2 long-handled wire baskets that
clip inside each other, available from gourmet
kitchen stores. Dip the larger wire basket in oil,
then line it completely and evenly with one-
fourth of the tangled noodles. Dip the smaller
wire basket in oil, then position it inside the
larger basket and clip it into position.

2 Heat 10 cm/4 inches of oil in a wok or deep-
fat fryer to 180–190°C/350–375°F, or until a
cube of bread browns in 30 seconds. Lower
the baskets into the oil and deep-fry for 2–3
minutes, or until the noodles are golden brown.
Remove the baskets from the oil and drain on
kitchen paper. Unclip the 2 wire baskets and
carefully remove the small one. Use a round-
bladed knife, if necessary, to prise the noodle
basket from the wire frame. Repeat to make
3 more baskets. Set aside to cool.

3 To make the salad, combine the sour
cream, mayonnaise, root ginger and lime rind.
Gradually add the lime juice until you get the
flavour you like. Stir in the chicken, carrot,
cucumber and seasoning to taste. Cover and
chill. Just before serving, stir in the herbs and
spoon the salad into the noodle baskets.

teriyaki chicken with sesame noodles

ingredients

SERVES 4

4 boneless chicken breasts,
    about 175 g/6 oz each,
    with or without skin, as
    you wish

about 4 tbsp bottled teriyaki
    sauce, or homemade
    teriyaki sauce

peanut or corn oil

sesame noodles

250 g/9 oz dried thin
    buckwheat noodles

1 tbsp toasted sesame oil

2 tbsp toasted sesame seeds

2 tbsp finely chopped fresh
    parsley

salt and pepper

method

1 Using a sharp knife, score each chicken breast diagonally across 3 times and rub all over with teriyaki sauce. Set aside to marinate for at least 10 minutes, or cover and chill all day.

2 When you are ready to cook the chicken, preheat the grill to high. Bring a saucepan of water to the boil, add the buckwheat noodles and boil for 3 minutes, until soft. Alternatively, cook according to the packet instructions. Drain and rinse well in cold water to stop the cooking and remove excess starch, then drain again.

3 Lightly brush the grill rack with oil. Add the chicken breasts, skin side up, and brush again with a little extra teriyaki sauce. Broil the chicken breasts about 10 cm/4 inches from the heat, brushing occasionally with extra teriyaki sauce, for 15 minutes, or until cooked through and the juices run clear.

4 Meanwhile, heat a wok over high heat. Add the sesame oil and heat until it shimmers. Add the noodles and stir round to heat through, then stir in the sesame seeds and parsley. Finally, add salt and pepper to taste.

5 Transfer the chicken breasts to plates and add a portion of noodles to each.

yaki soba

ingredients

SERVES 2

400 g/14 oz ramen noodles

1 onion, finely sliced

200 g/7 oz bean sprouts

1 red pepper, dedeseeded and finely shredded

1 boneless, skin-on cooked chicken breast, about 150 g/5^1/$_2$ oz, cooked and sliced

12 cooked peeled prawns

1 tbsp oil

2 tbsp shoyu (Japanese soy sauce)

^{1}/$_2$ tbsp mirin

1 tsp sesame oil

1 tsp roasted sesame seeds

2 spring onions, finely sliced

method

1 Cook the noodles according to the packet instructions, drain well, and tip into a bowl.

2 Mix the onion, bean sprouts, red pepper, chicken and prawns together in a separate bowl. Stir through the noodles.

3 Preheat a wok over high heat. Add the oil and heat until very hot. Add the noodle mixture and stir-fry for 4 minutes, or until golden, then add the shoyu, mirin and sesame oil and toss together.

4 Divide the mixture between 2 plates, sprinkle with the sesame seeds and spring onions and serve at once.

singapore noodles

ingredients

SERVES 4–6

300 g/10$\frac{1}{2}$ oz thin rice vermicelli

3 tbsp vegetable or peanut oil

2 garlic cloves, finely chopped

500 g/1 lb 2 oz small raw prawns, peeled, deveined and chopped into 2–3 pieces

115 g/4 oz cha siu, julienned

1 onion, finely sliced

1 tbsp mild curry powder, such as garam masala

1 green pepper, finely sliced

1 tsp sugar

1 tsp salt

1–2 tsp chicken stock

1 tbsp light soy sauce

200 g/7 oz bean sprouts, trimmed

method

1 Cook the rice vermicelli according to the directions on the packet. Drain and set aside.

2 In a preheated wok, heat 2 tablespoons of the oil. Toss in the garlic and stir-fry until fragrant. Add the prawns and stir-fry for 1 minute, or until the prawns are beginning to change colour. Add the cha siu and stir-fry for 1 more minute. Remove everything from the wok and set aside.

3 In the clean wok, heat the remaining oil. Add the onion and stir-fry for 1 minute, then stir in the curry powder. Add the pepper, sugar, salt and stock and stir-fry for 2 minutes. Pour in the light soy sauce followed by the vermicelli. Toss well. Finally, add the bean sprouts and the prawn-pork mixture. Stir until warmed through, then serve at once.

fish curry with rice noodles

ingredients

SERVES 4

2 tbsp vegetable or peanut oil

1 large onion, chopped

2 garlic cloves, chopped

85 g/3 oz white mushrooms

225 g/8 oz monkfish, cut into
    cubes, each about 1 inch

225 g/8 oz salmon fillets, cut
    into cubes, each about
    1 inch

225 g/8 oz cod, cut into
    cubes, each about 1 inch

2 tbsp Thai red curry paste

400 g/14 oz canned coconut
    milk

handful of fresh coriander,
    chopped

1 tsp jaggery or soft light
    brown sugar

1 tsp fish sauce

115 g/4 oz rice noodles

3 spring onions, chopped

50 g/2 oz bean sprouts

few Thai basil leaves

method

1 Heat the oil in a wok and gently sauté the onion, garlic and mushrooms until softened but not browned.

2 Add the fish, curry paste and coconut milk and bring gently to the boil. Simmer for 2–3 minutes before adding half the coriander, the sugar and the fish sauce. Keep warm.

3 Meanwhile, soak the noodles for 3–4 minutes (check the packet instructions) or until tender, and drain well through a colander. Put the colander and noodles over a pan of simmering water. Add the spring onions, bean sprouts and most of the basil and steam on top of the noodles for 1–2 minutes or until just wilted.

4 Pile the noodles onto warmed serving plates and top with the fish curry. Sprinkle the remaining coriander and basil over the top and serve immediately.

stir-fried noodles with marinated fish

ingredients

SERVES 4

450 g/1 lb monkfish or cod, cubed

225 g/8 oz salmon fillets, cubed

2 tbsp vegetable or peanut oil

2 fresh green chillies, deseeded and chopped

grated rind and juice of 1 lime

1 tbsp fish sauce

115 g/4 oz wide rice noodles

2 tbsp vegetable or peanut oil

2 shallots, sliced

2 garlic cloves, chopped finely

1 fresh red chilli, deseeded and chopped

2 tbsp Thai soy sauce

2 tbsp chilli sauce

method

1 Place the fish in a shallow bowl. To make the marinade, mix the oil, green chillies, lime juice and rind and fish sauce together and pour over the fish. Cover and chill for 2 hours.

2 Put the noodles in a bowl and cover with boiling water. Leave for 8–10 minutes (check the packet instructions) and drain well.

3 Heat the oil in a wok and sauté the shallots, garlic and red chilli until lightly browned. Add the soy sauce and chilli sauce. Add the fish and the marinade to the wok and stir-fry gently for 2–3 minutes until cooked through.

4 Add the drained noodles and stir gently. Sprinkle with coriander and serve immediately.

curried noodles with prawns & straw mushrooms

ingredients

SERVES 4

1 tbsp vegetable or peanut oil

3 shallots, chopped

1 fresh red chilli, deseeded
    and chopped

1 tbsp Thai red curry paste

1 lemon grass stalk (white
    part only), chopped finely

225 g/8 oz cooked peeled
    prawns

400 g/14 oz canned straw
    mushrooms, drained

2 tbsp fish sauce

2 tbsp Thai soy sauce

225 g/8 oz fresh egg noodles

fresh coriander, chopped,
    to garnish

method

1 Heat the oil in a wok and stir-fry the shallots
and chilli for 2–3 minutes. Add the curry paste
and lemon grass and stir-fry for 2–3 minutes.

2 Add the prawns, mushrooms, fish sauce
and soy sauce and stir well to mix.

3 Meanwhile, cook the noodles in boiling
water for 3–4 minutes, drain and transfer to
warmed plates. Top with the prawn curry,
sprinkle the coriander over and serve at once.

spicy noodles with mushroom egg rolls

ingredients

SERVES 4

2 tbsp vegetable or peanut oil

1 small onion, chopped finely

225 g/8 oz mushrooms, chopped

1 tbsp Thai red curry paste

1 tbsp Thai soy sauce

1 tbsp fish sauce

8 square egg roll skins

vegetable or peanut oil, for deep-frying

225 g/8 oz quick-cook noodles

1 garlic clove, chopped

6 spring onions, chopped

1 red pepper, deseeded and chopped

1 tbsp ground coriander

1 tbsp ground cumin

method

1 Heat 1 tablespoon of the oil in a wok and stir-fry the onion and mushrooms until crisp and browned. Add the curry paste, soy sauce and fish sauce and stir-fry for 2–3 minutes. Remove the wok from the heat.

2 Spoon an eighth of the mixture across one of the egg roll skins and roll up, folding the sides over the filling to enclose it.

3 Heat the oil for deep-frying in a wok and deep-fry the egg rolls, 4 at a time, until crisp and browned. Drain on kitchen paper and keep warm.

4 Meanwhile, put the noodles in a bowl, cover with boiling water and set aside to swell.

5 Heat the remaining oil in the wok and stir-fry the garlic, spring onions and red pepper for 2–3 minutes. Stir in the coriander and cumin, then drain the noodles and add them to the wok. Toss together and serve topped with the egg rolls.

vegetarian

The cuisine of Eastern and Southeastern Asia, with its wonderful array of fresh vegetables, is perfectly suited to the vegetarian diet and wok cookery is the ideal way to ensure that the important nutrients are retained.

There is no dairy produce in this region, so cheese, a typical source of protein used in a vegetarian diet, is absent from these recipes. Instead, the protein is provided by nuts – try some delicious, vibrantly coloured vegetables with roasted cashew nuts, made special by the addition of a sweet-and-sour sauce – and by tofu. This is a curious but exceptionally nutritious food made from soy beans in a similar way to cheese. It usually comes in a slab, which can be cut into cubes, and has a completely bland taste that readily takes on flavour, making it ideal to use in curries and stir-fries. Try Spicy Tofu – the tofu will soak up the chilli, garlic and ginger flavours and if you've never tried it before, you will be converted!

These recipes also make excellent side dishes to accompany Asian dishes. Try some of the simple stir-fried vegetables as an accompaniment to rich meat dishes – for example, the Stir-fried Bean sprouts, Chinese Greens, and Long Beans with Red Pepper would make an attractive selection. Good health!

aubergine with miso

ingredients

SERVES 4

2 aubergines

oil, for stir-frying

1 fresh red chilli, sliced

2 tbsp sake

4 tbsp mirin

2 tbsp shoyu (Japanese
    soy sauce)

3 tbsp hatcho miso

2 tbsp water

method

1 Cut the aubergines into wedges.

2 Preheat a wok over high heat. Add a little oil and heat until very hot. Stir-fry the aubergine, in batches, for 4 minutes, or until browned and cooked through.

3 Return all the aubergine to the wok together with the chilli and stir together. Add the remaining ingredients and toss everything together. Cook, stirring, until the sauce thickens. Serve immediately.

aubergine with red peppers

ingredients

SERVES 4

3 tbsp vegetable or peanut oil

1 garlic clove, finely chopped

3 aubergines, halved
    lengthways and cut
    diagonally into
    2.5-cm/1-inch pieces

1 tsp white rice vinegar

1 red pepper, finely sliced

2 tbsp light soy sauce

1 tsp sugar

1 tbsp finely chopped
    coriander leaves, to
    garnish

method

1 In a preheated wok, heat the oil. When it begins to smoke, toss in the garlic and stir-fry until fragrant, then add the aubergine pieces. Stir-fry for 30 seconds, then add the vinegar. Turn down the heat and cook, covered, for 5 minutes, stirring occasionally.

2 When the aubergine pieces are soft, add the pepper and stir. Add the light soy sauce and sugar and cook, uncovered, for 2 minutes.

3 Remove from the heat and stand for 2 minutes. Transfer to a dish, then garnish with chopped coriander and serve.

mixed vegetables with quick-fried basil

ingredients

SERVES 4

2 tbsp vegetable or peanut oil

2 garlic cloves, chopped

1 onion, sliced

115 g/4 oz baby corn cobs,
    cut in half diagonally

1/2 cucumber, peeled, halved,
    deseeded and sliced

225 g/8 oz canned water
    chestnuts, drained
    and rinsed

55 g/2 oz mangetout,
    trimmed

115 g/4 oz shiitake
    mushrooms, halved

1 red pepper, deseeded and
    sliced thinly

1 tbsp jaggery or soft light
    brown sugar

2 tbsp Thai soy sauce

1 tbsp fish sauce

1 tbsp rice vinegar

boiled rice, to serve

quick-fried basil

vegetable or peanut oil,
    for cooking

8–12 sprigs fresh Thai basil

method

1 Heat the oil in a wok and stir-fry the garlic and onion for 1–2 minutes. Add the corn cobs, cucumber, water chestnuts, mangetout, mushrooms and red pepper and stir-fry for 2–3 minutes, until starting to soften.

2 Add the sugar, soy sauce, fish sauce and vinegar and gradually bring to the boil. Simmer for 1–2 minutes.

3 Meanwhile, heat the oil for the basil in a wok and, when hot, add the basil sprigs. Cook for 20–30 seconds, until crisp. Remove with a slotted spoon and drain on kitchen paper.

4 Garnish the vegetable stir-fry with the crispy basil and serve immediately, with the boiled rice.

sweet-&-sour vegetables with cashew nuts

ingredients

SERVES 4

1 tbsp vegetable or peanut oil

1 tsp chilli oil

2 onions, sliced

2 carrots, sliced thinly

2 courgettes, sliced thinly

115 g/4 oz head of broccoli,
cut into florets

115 g/4 oz white mushrooms,
sliced

115 g/4 oz small pak choi,
halved

2 tbsp jaggery or soft light
brown sugar

2 tbsp Thai soy sauce

1 tbsp rice vinegar

55 g/2 oz cashew nuts

method

1 Heat the vegetable or peanut oil and the chilli oil in a wok and stir-fry the onions for 1–2 minutes, until they start to soften.

2 Add the carrots, courgettes and broccoli, and stir-fry for 2–3 minutes. Add the mushrooms, pak choi, sugar, soy sauce and rice vinegar and stir-fry for 1–2 minutes.

3 Meanwhile, dry-fry or toast the cashew nuts. Sprinkle the cashews over the stir-fry and serve immediately.

hot-&-sour cabbage

ingredients

SERVES 4

450 g/1 lb firm white cabbage

1 tbsp vegetable or peanut oil

10 Sichuan peppers or more,
    to taste

3 dried chillies, roughly
    chopped

$^1/_2$ tsp salt

1 tsp white rice vinegar

dash of sesame oil

pinch of sugar

method

1 To prepare the cabbage, discard the outer leaves and tough stems. Chop the cabbage into 3-cm/1$^1/_4$-inch squares, breaking up the chunks. Rinse thoroughly in cold water.

2 In a preheated wok, heat the oil and cook the peppers until fragrant. Stir in the chillies. Throw in the cabbage, a little at a time, together with the salt and stir-fry for 2 minutes.

3 Add the vinegar, sesame oil and sugar and cook for a further minute, or until the cabbage is tender. Serve immediately.

spicy green beans

ingredients

SERVES 4

200 g/7 oz green beans,
　　trimmed and cut
　　diagonally into 3–4 pieces

2 tbsp vegetable or peanut oil

4 dried chillies, cut into
　　2 or 3 pieces

$1/2$ tsp Sichuan peppers

1 garlic clove, finely sliced

6 thin slices of fresh root
　　ginger

2 spring onions, white part
　　only, cut diagonally into
　　thin pieces

pinch of sea salt

method

1 Blanch the beans in a large pan of boiling water for 30 seconds. Drain and set aside.

2 In a preheated wok, heat 1 tablespoon of the oil. Over low heat, stir-fry the beans for about 5 minutes, or until they are beginning to wrinkle. Remove and set aside.

3 Add the remaining oil and stir-fry the chillies and peppers until they are fragrant. Add the garlic, root ginger and spring onions and stir-fry until they begin to soften. Throw in the beans and toss to mix, then add the sea salt and serve immediately.

cauliflower & beans with cashew nuts

ingredients

SERVES 4

1 tbsp vegetable or peanut oil

1 tbsp chilli oil

1 onion, chopped

2 garlic cloves, chopped

2 tbsp Thai red curry paste

1 small cauliflower, cut into
   florets

175 g/6 oz runner beans,
   cut into 7.5-cm/3-inch
   lengths

150 ml/5 fl oz vegetable stock

2 tbsp Thai soy sauce

50 g/1³/₄ oz toasted cashew
   nuts, to garnish

method

1 Heat both the oils in a wok and stir-fry the onion and garlic until softened. Add the curry paste and stir-fry for 1–2 minutes.

2 Add the cauliflower and beans and stir-fry for 3–4 minutes, until softened. Pour in the stock and soy sauce and simmer for 1–2 minutes. Serve immediately, garnished with the cashew nuts.

julienne vegetable salad

ingredients

SERVES 4

4 tbsp vegetable or peanut oil

225 g/8 oz tofu with herbs, cubed

1 red onion, sliced

4 spring onions, cut into 5-cm/2-inch lengths

1 garlic clove, chopped

2 carrots, cut into short, thin sticks

115 g/4 oz fine green beans, trimmed

1 yellow pepper, deseeded and cut into strips

115 g/4 oz head of broccoli, cut into florets

1 large courgette, cut into short, thin sticks

55 g/2 oz bean sprouts

2 tbsp Thai red curry paste

4 tbsp Thai soy sauce

1 tbsp rice wine vinegar

1 tsp jaggery or soft light brown sugar

few Thai basil leaves

350 g/12 oz rice vermicelli noodles

method

1 Heat the oil in a wok and cook the tofu cubes for 3–4 minutes, until browned on all sides. Lift the cubes out of the oil and drain on kitchen paper.

2 Add the onions, garlic and carrots to the hot oil and cook for 1–2 minutes before adding the rest of the vegetables, except for the bean sprouts. Stir-fry for 2–3 minutes. Add the bean sprouts, then stir in the curry paste, soy, vinegar, sugar and basil leaves. Cook for 30 seconds.

3 Soak the noodles in boiling water or stock for 2–3 minutes (check the packet instructions) or until tender and drain well.

4 Pile the vegetables onto the noodles, and serve topped with the tofu cubes. Garnish with extra basil if desired.

oyster mushrooms & vegetables with peanut chilli sauce

ingredients

SERVES 4

1 tbsp sesame oil

4 spring onions, sliced finely

1 carrot, cut into batons

1 courgette, cut into batons

1/2 head of broccoli,
    cut into florets

450 g/1 lb oyster mushrooms,
    sliced thinly

2 tbsp crunchy peanut butter

1 tsp chilli powder, or to taste

3 tbsp water

cooked rice or noodles,
    to serve

wedges of lime, to garnish

method

1 Heat the oil in a wok until almost smoking. Stir-fry the spring onions for 1 minute. Add the carrot and courgette and stir-fry for another minute. Then add the broccoli and cook for one more minute.

2 Stir in the mushrooms and cook until they are soft and at least half the liquid they produce has evaporated. Add the peanut butter and stir well. Season with the chilli powder to taste. Finally, add the water and cook for one more minute.

3 Serve over rice or noodles and garnish with wedges of lime.

broccoli & mangetout stir-fry

ingredients

SERVES 4

2 tbsp vegetable or peanut oil

dash of sesame oil

1 garlic clove, finely chopped

225 g/8 oz small head of
  broccoli florets

115 g/4 oz mangetout,
  trimmed

225 g/8 oz Chinese leaves,
  chopped into 1-cm/
  $1/2$-inch slices

5–6 spring onions, finely
  chopped

$1/2$ tsp salt

2 tbsp light soy sauce

1 tbsp Shaoxing rice wine

1 tsp sesame seeds, lightly
  toasted

method

1 In a preheated wok, heat the oils, then add the garlic and stir-fry vigorously. Add all the vegetables and salt and stir-fry over high heat, tossing rapidly, for about 3 minutes.

2 Pour in the light soy sauce and Shaoxing and cook for a further 2 minutes. Sprinkle with the sesame seeds and serve hot.

stir-fried long beans with red pepper

ingredients

SERVES 4–6

280 g/10 oz long beans, cut
   into 6-cm/2^1/$_2$-inch lengths

1 tbsp vegetable or peanut oil

1 red pepper, slivered

pinch of salt

pinch of sugar

method

1 Blanch the beans in a large pan of boiling water for 30 seconds. Drain and set aside.

2 In a preheated wok, heat the oil and stir-fry the beans for 1 minute over high heat. Add the pepper and stir-fry for 1 more minute. Sprinkle the salt and sugar on top and serve.

spicy vegetarian stir-fry

ingredients

SERVES 4

3 tbsp vegetable oil

$^1/_2$ tsp turmeric

salt and pepper

225 g/8 oz potatoes, cut into
  1-cm/$^1/_2$-inch cubes

3 shallots, chopped finely

1 bay leaf

$^1/_2$ tsp ground cumin

1 tsp finely grated fresh
  root ginger

$^1/_4$ tsp chilli powder

4 tomatoes, chopped coarsely

300 g/10$^1/_2$ oz spinach
  (de-stalked), chopped
  roughly

125 g/4$^1/_2$ oz fresh or frozen
  peas

1 tbsp lemon juice

cooked basmati rice, to serve

method

1 In a wok, heat 2 tablespoons of the oil and add the turmeric and a pinch of salt. Carefully add the potatoes, stirring continuously to coat in the turmeric. Stir-fry for 5 minutes, then remove from the wok and set aside.

2 Heat the remaining tablespoon of oil and stir-fry the shallots for 1–2 minutes. Mix in the bay leaf, cumin, root ginger and chilli powder, then add the tomatoes and stir-fry for 2 minutes.

3 Add the spinach, mixing well to combine all the flavours. Cover and simmer for 2–3 minutes. Return the potatoes to the wok and add the peas and lemon juice. Cook for 5 minutes, or until the potatoes are tender.

4 Remove the wok from the heat and discard the bay leaf, then season with salt and pepper. Serve with cooked basmati rice.

stir-fried chinese greens

ingredients

SERVES 4

1 tbsp vegetable or peanut oil

1 tsp finely chopped garlic

225 g/8 oz leafy Chinese
leaves, roughly chopped

$1/2$ tsp salt

method

1 In a preheated wok, heat the oil and stir-fry the garlic until fragrant. Over high heat, toss in the Chinese leaves and salt and stir-fry for 1 minute maximum. Serve immediately.

stir-fried bean sprouts

ingredients

SERVES 4

1 tbsp vegetable or peanut oil

225 g/8 oz bean sprouts, trimmed

2 tbsp finely chopped spring onion

$^1/_2$ tsp salt

pinch of sugar

method

1 In a preheated wok, heat the oil and stir-fry the bean sprouts with the spring onion for about 1 minute. Add the salt and sugar and stir.

2 Serve immediately.

aubergine & bean curry

ingredients

SERVES 4

2 tbsp vegetable or peanut oil

1 onion, chopped

2 garlic cloves, crushed

2 fresh red chillies, deseeded
and chopped

1 tbsp Thai red curry paste

1 large aubergine, cut into
chunks

115 g/4 oz pea or small
aubergines

115 g/4 oz baby broad beans

115 g/4 oz fine green beans

300 ml/10 fl oz vegetable
stock

55 g/2 oz block creamed
coconut, chopped

3 tbsp Thai soy sauce

1 tsp jaggery or soft light
brown sugar

3 kaffir lime leaves, torn
coarsely

4 tbsp chopped fresh
coriander

method

1 Heat the oil in a wok and sauté the onion, garlic and chillies for 1–2 minutes. Stir in the curry paste and cook for 1–2 minutes.

2 Add the aubergines and cook for 3–4 minutes, until starting to soften. (You may need to add a little more oil as aubergines soak it up quickly.) Add all the beans and stir-fry for 2 minutes.

3 Pour in the stock and add the creamed coconut, soy sauce, sugar and lime leaves. Bring gently to the boil and cook until the coconut has dissolved. Stir in the coriander and serve hot.

onion, potato & red pepper curry

ingredients

SERVES 4

2 tbsp vegetable or peanut oil

2 red onions, sliced

2 garlic cloves, chopped finely

2-inch piece fresh root ginger, chopped finely

1 fresh red chilli, deseeded and chopped

1 tbsp Thai red curry paste

225 g/8 oz potatoes, cut into cubes, boiled for 5 minutes and drained

2 red peppers, deseeded and diced

300 ml/10 fl oz vegetable stock

1 tsp salt

4 tbsp chopped fresh coriander

method

1 Heat the oil in a wok and stir-fry the onions, garlic, root ginger and chilli for 2–3 minutes. Add the curry paste and stir-fry over low heat for 2–3 minutes.

2 Add the potatoes, peppers, stock and salt and cook for 3–4 minutes, until all the vegetables are tender. Stir in the coriander and serve immediately.

courgette & cashew nut curry

ingredients

SERVES 4

2 tbsp vegetable or peanut oil

6 spring onions, chopped

2 garlic cloves, chopped

2 fresh green chillies,
    deseeded and chopped

450 g/1 lb courgettes, cut into
    thick slices

115 g/4 oz shiitake
    mushrooms, halved

55 g/2 oz bean sprouts

75 g/2¾ oz cashew nuts,
    toasted or dry-fried

few Chinese chives, chopped

4 tbsp Thai soy sauce

1 tsp fish sauce

rice or noodles, to serve

method

1 Heat the oil in a wok and sauté the spring onions, garlic and chillies for 1–2 minutes, until softened but not browned.

2 Add the courgettes and mushrooms and cook for 2–3 minutes until tender.

3 Add the bean sprouts, nuts, chives and both sauces and stir-fry for 1–2 minutes.

4 Serve hot with rice or noodles.

tofu & green vegetable curry

ingredients

SERVES 4

vegetable or peanut oil,
    for deep-frying
225 g/8 oz firm tofu, cut into
    cubes
2 tbsp vegetable or peanut oil
1 tbsp chilli oil
2 fresh green chillies,
    deseeded and sliced
2 garlic cloves, crushed
6 spring onions, sliced
2 medium courgettes,
    cut into sticks
$^{1}/_{2}$ cucumber, peeled,
    deseeded and sliced
1 green pepper, deseeded
    and sliced
1 small head of broccoli, cut
    into florets
55 g/2 oz fine green beans,
    halved
55 g/2 oz frozen peas, thawed
300 ml/10 fl oz vegetable
    stock
55 g/2 oz block creamed
    coconut, chopped
2 tbsp Thai soy sauce
1 tsp soft light brown sugar
4 tbsp chopped fresh parsley,
    to garnish

method

1 Heat the oil for deep-frying in a wok and carefully lower in the tofu cubes, in batches, and cook for 2–3 minutes, until golden brown. Remove with a slotted spoon and drain on kitchen paper.

2 Heat the other oils in a wok and stir-fry the chillies, garlic and spring onions for 2–3 minutes. Add the courgettes, cucumber, green pepper, broccoli and green beans, and stir-fry for a further 2–3 minutes.

3 Add the peas, stock, coconut, soy sauce and sugar. Cover and simmer for 2–3 minutes, until all the vegetables are tender and the coconut has dissolved.

4 Stir in the tofu and serve immediately, sprinkled with the parsley.

agedashi tofu

ingredients

SERVES 2

150 ml/5 fl oz water

2 tsp dashi granules

2 tbsp shoyu (Japanese
    soy sauce)

2 tbsp mirin

vegetable oil, for deep-frying

300 g/10¹/₂ oz silken tofu,
    drained on kitchen paper
    and cut into 4 cubes

2 tbsp plain flour

1 tsp grated fresh root ginger

2 tsp grated daikon

¹/₄ tsp kezuri-bushi shavings

method

1 Put the water in a pan with the dashi granules and bring to the boil. Add the shoyu and mirin and cook for 1 minute. Keep warm.

2 Preheat a wok, then fill one-third full with oil, or use a deep-fryer. Heat the oil to 180–190°C/350–375°F, or until a cube of bread browns in 30 seconds. Meanwhile, dust the tofu cubes with the flour.

3 Add the tofu pieces to the oil, in batches, and cook until lightly golden in colour. Remove, drain on kitchen paper and keep hot while you cook the remaining tofu cubes.

4 Put 2 pieces of tofu in each of 2 bowls and divide the dashi stock between them. Top with root ginger, daikon and kezuri-bushi.

vegetables with tofu & spinach

ingredients

SERVES 4

vegetable or peanut oil, for
    deep-frying

225 g/8 oz firm tofu, drained
    and cut into cubes

2 tbsp vegetable or peanut oil

2 onions, chopped

2 garlic cloves, chopped

1 fresh red chilli, deseeded
    and sliced

3 celery stalks, sliced
    diagonally

225 g/8 oz mushrooms,
    sliced thickly

115 g/4 oz baby corn cobs,
    cut in half

1 red pepper, deseeded and
    cut into strips

3 tbsp Thai red curry paste

400 g/14 oz coconut milk

1 tsp jaggery or soft light
    brown sugar

2 tbsp Thai soy sauce

225 g/8 oz baby spinach
    leaves

method

1 Heat the oil in a wok and deep-fry the tofu cubes, in batches, for 4–5 minutes, until crisp and browned. Remove with a slotted spoon and drain on kitchen paper.

2 Heat 2 tablespoons of the oil in a wok and stir-fry the onions, garlic and chilli for 1–2 minutes, until they start to soften. Add the celery, mushrooms, corn cobs and red pepper, and stir-fry for 3–4 minutes, until they soften.

3 Stir in the curry paste and coconut milk and gradually bring to the boil. Add the sugar and soy sauce and then the spinach. Cook, stirring constantly, until the spinach has wilted. Serve immediately, topped with the tofu.

bamboo shoots with tofu

ingredients

SERVES 4–6

3 dried Chinese mushrooms,
    soaked in warm water
    for 20 minutes

55 g/2 oz baby pak choi

vegetable or peanut oil,
    for deep-frying

450 g/1 lb firm tofu, cut into
    2.5-cm/1-inch squares

115 g/4 oz fresh or canned
    bamboo shoots, rinsed
    and finely sliced (if using
    fresh shoots, boil in water
    first for 30 minutes)

1 tsp oyster sauce

1 tsp light soy sauce

method

1 Squeeze out any excess water from the mushrooms and finely slice, discarding any tough stems. Blanch the pak choi in a large pan of boiling water for 30 seconds. Drain and set aside.

2 Heat enough oil for deep-frying in a wok or deep-fat fryer until it reaches 180–190°C/350–375°F, or until a cube of bread browns in 30 seconds. Cook the tofu cubes until golden brown. Remove, then drain and set aside.

3 In a preheated wok, heat 1 tablespoon of the oil, then toss in the mushrooms and pak choi and stir. Add the tofu and bamboo shoots with the oyster and soy sauces. Heat through and serve.

spicy tofu

ingredients

SERVES 4

marinade

75 ml/2¹/₂ fl oz vegetable
    bouillon

2 tsp cornflour

2 tbsp soy sauce

1 tbsp caster sugar

pinch of chilli flakes

stir-fry

250 g/9 oz firm tofu, rinsed
    and drained thoroughly
    and cut into 1 cm/
    ¹/₂ inch cubes

4 tbsp peanut oil

1 tbsp grated fresh root ginger

3 garlic cloves, crushed

4 spring onions, sliced thinly

1 head of broccoli, cut
    into florets

1 carrot, cut into batons

1 yellow pepper, sliced thinly

250 g/9 oz shiitake
    mushrooms, sliced thinly

steamed rice, to serve

method

1 Blend the vegetable bouillon, cornflour, soy sauce, sugar and chilli flakes together in a large bowl. Add the tofu and toss well to coat. Set aside to marinate for 20 minutes.

2 In a wok, heat 2 tablespoons of the peanut oil and stir-fry the tofu with its marinade until brown and crispy. Remove from the wok and set aside.

3 Heat the remaining 2 tablespoons of peanut oil in the wok and stir-fry the root ginger, garlic and spring onions for 30 seconds. Add the broccoli, carrot, yellow pepper and mushrooms to the wok and cook for 5–6 minutes. Return the tofu to the wok and stir-fry to reheat. Serve immediately over steamed rice.